The Redd Foxx Encyclopedia
of Black Humor

The Redd Foxx
Encyclopedia
of Black Humor

Redd Foxx and Norma Miller

Ward Ritchie Press
Pasadena, California

Wit and humor

To all those fine black men and women who have dedicated their lives to making others laugh away hundreds of years of sorrow, grief, and misery.

We could not have created this book without the combined efforts of Bill Chleboun, Executive Editor of Ward Ritchie Press, and our friend and manager, Julian Portman —who while sipping a "shooter" developed the idea for this book. We also wish to thank Joe X. Price, one of Hollywood's top writers, for his contributions.

I, Norma Miller, would like to thank my co-author, Redd Foxx, for his faith and trust in me as a person, for teaching me his art, and for helping other people to enjoy comedy from a comedienne. I also wish to thank my family for all their years of understanding and love.

I, Redd Foxx, wish to state without a smile, a laugh, applause, what is there for a performer? To those men who disagree, I wish them one thing, a perpetual soft-on.

PREFACE

Black humor, what is it? For that matter, what is white humor? Italian humor? Jewish humor? What do they all have in common? All of these ethnic groups were born out of one tragedy or another. The black people came out of their slave background, the Italian people out of an emotional oppression, and the Jewish people out of a religious and social persecution. Whenever an oppressed people are without the ability to improve their situation, they begin to laugh at themselves and make jokes about their situation. It is only when people can laugh at themselves that they become human beings. Nothing makes people more human than when they are laughing at themselves.

Why do we laugh? We laugh at something because it looks funny or at something funny that someone said. There are many different reasons why we laugh, and in show business we are constantly trying to cause this reaction. The two symbols of the theater are the masks of comedy and tragedy. Although these two emotions seem to be at opposite poles, they are quite often closely related. A particular event that triggers a response of laughter can at a different time or under different circumstances, create a tearful response.

We have all experienced the time when laughter reaches a high degree of intensity and, at the same time, the tear ducts begin to work for a different reason.

In the royal courts of Europe, kings kept court jesters for the purpose of having instant amusement for them and the other members of the court. This closely resembles the situation today at a typical television taping session, when the audience is told when to laugh and when to applaud during the program. Although there are many differences between people—from color, to language, to size—and they may do things in different ways, there is always one thing that they all do: they laugh. It becomes the common denominator that binds all people.

Slavery was the black man's burden; however, it was this same slave burden that gave him his source of material to create black humor. Here is a typical case of laughter and tragedy. The tragedy of slavery was the reason for the laughter of the clown. One can imagine the master watching his slaves perform and saying, "That's a funny nigger!" Although there have been many changes in our society since that time, that comment can still be heard in Las Vegas today, spoken by the white man who has just seen me, Redd Foxx, perform. In a practical sense, these two emotions are as close as love and hate; yet they have played an important role in the development of black humor.

This book is dedicated to those funny men who made the world richer because they laughed at themselves. They sang the songs that tore at your heart strings; they played the music that you could tap your feet to; and they enriched the lives of black people and made them proud to be black. To these funny men and women we say, "Right on! Keep doing your thing. Keep on trucking because you gave the world what it needs the most, laughter!"

CONTENTS

PLANTATION SHOWS

PLANTATION SHOWS

Music played a large role in the survival of the black people in America—that and a sense of humor that just couldn't be enslaved. While many immigrants of varying ethnic backgrounds complained bitterly about having been forced by circumstances and finances to cross the Atlantic in sweltering steerage, they at least made the trip voluntarily. Many were fleeing oppressors, but they escaped. And after having encountered all manner of degradation at the hands of unfeeling immigration officials, they left Ellis Island free people—free to seek their fortunes in a bright new land.

Not so our native African brothers and sisters. First brought here by slavers in 1619, they had been rounded up from various African nations, herded into slave-ship holds that made European immigrant steerage seem first class, and afforded even less freedom and dignity than the cattle they were being treated like. Shackled at the neck, wrists, and ankles, they languished in the bowels of the slavers' ships until hauled deckside for an hour or two of vigorous daily exercise. Then they were flung back into the stench of their ocean-going prisons.

Once ashore in what others considered the promised land, those Africans who survived the treacherous crossing didn't have to go through the humiliation of a U.S. Customs—they were sent straight to the auction block, where they were merchandise to be bought and sold, traded and loaned, and they went only when and where their owners told them to. This was their welcome to the land of opportunity, being purchased by southern plantation gentry of British heritage, who promptly put them to work.

While the European newcomers were handicapped by a language barrier, they had hope. Most spoke languages with alphabets and sounds not too far from English, so they soon understood enough to get by on—and they had their families and friends to speak with in their native tongue whenever they felt homesick.

PLANTATION SHOWS

The Africans, on the other hand, were not so fortunate there, either. Having been uprooted from many different tribes throughout Africa and torn from their families and other members of their tribe, they found it impossible to communicate even with the persons chained to either side of them. And the English spoken by the slavers and sailors was even more foreign, as were their ways.

The only thing the captives had going for them was their music and their unflagging humor. Through song and dance they could communicate, tell a story, explain their feelings, vent their frustrations, show their hope. The one thing they all had in common was a foot-stomping, hand-clapping rhythm and chant. Even though they didn't understand one another's tongue, they understood the beat and the musical sounds, and that made them feel a little more secure. Once a method of communication had been established, they felt more at home with these other Africans, who looked so much like themselves but who just couldn't talk their language, even if they were allowed. But slaves were forbidden to speak their native tongue.

Soon singing and dancing became an integral part of the slaves' recreation, an outlet for their emotions and a relief from the hard day's labor from sunup to sundown. The fieldhands, especially, joined in the merriment to help unwind from their back-breaking work. Forming a semi-circle in the cool of the southern evening, they would take turns entertaining one another. From basic clapping and chanting, they progressed to more sophisticated dancing and singing, imitating their white masters' walk and airs.

The plantation owners were highly amused by their "darkies'" antics and wondered at their never-ending good humor and energy. Little did the masters know that a great deal of what the slaves were communicating was their feelings about their oppressive owners. They strutted and pranced, mocking the cockiness they saw in their white "betters." And when they dressed up in their masters'

PLANTATION SHOWS

hand-me-downs and danced around the semicircle in the glow of the moonlight, the whites could only shake their heads in fond amazement at these seemingly childlike "nigras" who always appeared to be so happy.

Before long, the slaves were speaking English, or rather, a form of it. What they heard their masters say, which was usually laced with a British accent—and often slurred by the effects of heat and alcohol—they combined with the sounds of their native tongue and came up with an original sound. In one of Redd Foxx's routines, he speaks of the African learning to talk English by listening to the southern white man: "Hey, boy. Bring dat dere yonder. Chunk it, nigger, chunk it." The African responds by saying: "Ooba gooba," which, when translated, means: "Chunk that shit yo'self!"

Once they all spoke the same pidgin English, they were able to communicate both with their masters and with one another. Since their masters could only understand them to a small degree, they developed a method of communication through double meaning and body language that was unknown to the whites. Thus, when they sang their spirituals, they were not merely praying for the white man's god to deliver them from sin and help them attain peace in the hereafter; they were asking for a whole lot more. Their spirituals were really protest songs. Under the blazing sun, a group of workers would sing:

Steal away, steal away, steal away to Jesus;
Steal away, steal away, Lord
I ain't got long to stay here.

In the next field, another batch of slaves would answer:

Swing low, sweet chariot,
Comin' for to carry me home;
Swing low, sweet chariot,
Comin' for to carry me home.

PLANTATION SHOWS

While the masters thought they were singing about their eventual death and deliverance and were just singing to while away the hours in the fields, the slaves were actually letting one another know that the underground railroad was leaving that evening. The workers were singing about the fact that they didn't have long to stay there, and underground railroad meant "by foot." They were going to take the first thing smoking out of there—even if it "weren't nuthin' but a nigger with a pipe."

Blacks took to religion, the white man's religion, probably because they felt that if they prayed hard enough and loud enough to the white man's god, maybe it would help them understand what was happening to them. It also gave them an outlet for their double-meaning songs. When they embraced the Old Testament and sang their slave spirituals, they were really talking about themselves:

Go down, Moses, way down in Egypt land,
Let my people go.
Oppressed so hard they could not stand,
Let my people go.
Go down, Moses, way down to Egypt land,
Tell old Pharaoh to let my people go.

They identified with the plight of the Israelites and sang of being set free. But since they couldn't very well sing of their own freedom, they masked their intent slyly with songs about Israelites, cleverly making their songs inoffensively religious in nature.

The River Jordan runs deeply through their songs, since they saw it as the dividing line between them and the promised land—their freedom. In the Bible, and thus safely spoken of aloud, the river they yearned to cross was always on their minds. The river also symbolized the waters they had crossed in getting to their enslavement. They didn't know where they were or who they were, or what was going to become of them, but they did remember

they had crossed a very wide "river." They longed to cross it once more.

There were basically two types of slaves, and both were very good mimics. The house slaves were excellent mimes and imitated their masters' mannerisms so well that they came off as uppity as any snobs could be. They felt themselves to be superior to the rest of the slaves and looked down their noses at the fieldhands. The field workers, also very good mimes, became the first black entertainers, patterning their speech after their bosses' slurred delivery when in the fields.

Besides singing and dancing, they had their laughter. By acting the fool, the clown, and by bucking their eyes and cackling when they laughed, they evoked laughter from their audiences. They also got laughs from imitating everything and anybody they had come in contact with since their arrival on the plantation. And to make their shows complete, they even invented their own musical instruments.

They made banjos out of cheese boxes with tanned ground-hog skins stretched tightly over them or out of pigs' bladders tied with a string. Gumbo boxes were made with sheepskin. A form of drum was created by covering a wine cask with cowhide and beating on it with hollowed-out dried beef bones. Around their ankles they wore small bamboo sticks that clicked as they moved their feet. They shook dried animal jawbones so the teeth rattled in their sockets, and they forged crude triangles that, when clicked together, made castanets.

Thus prepared, the musical slaves became the official entertainers of the South. They achieved a higher status through their new talents and extended it by creating the image of the lazy black coon—baggy pants, floppy shoes, and all. Their desire to entertain was not so strong as their desire to keep out of the fields. By becoming amusing darkies, who entertained the master and his guests, they found themselves a new identity and a way out of the field.

PLANTATION SHOWS

Having lost their heritage, language, and customs, they had to be content with whatever they could become. Some of them became so successful at performing for their masters and the guests that the masters would book their talented slaves out to other plantations as entertainers. These slaves were the first standup comedians.

It's not really clear when plantation minstrel shows actually began; their history is sketchy at best, since there were no official records kept. There is, however, a water-color painting, done by an unknown artist, hanging in the Ludwell Paradine House in Williamsburg, Virginia that is dated 1790 and titled The Old Plantation. It clearly shows a group of slaves standing by a cabin and being entertained by a banjo player, a drummer, and some dancers. It is a rare portrait of slaves doing their wedding-ritual stick dance accompanied by drum and stringed instrument.

An even earlier portrayal of performing slaves was created by Long Island artist William S. Mount. Dated 1785, his paintings—The Banjo Player, A Spoon Player, and The Fiddler—captured the authentic look of the beginning minstrel days of the plantation shows.

In 1838, British actress Fanny Kemble wrote of slave entertainers in her Journal of Life on a Georgia Plantation: "They always keep exquisite time and tune and no words seem too hard for them to adapt to their tunes, so that they can sing a long-metre hymn to a short-metre tune without difficulty . . . with the most perfect time." She seemed quite impressed with their sense of rhythm.

While some black entertainers were used merely to while away an otherwise boring evening, others were considered cash assets. Three Louisville slaves were valued so highly that in 1844 their master estimated their value at $1,500 apiece. When the three musicians took off for the North, their master spent several thousands of dollars trying to retrieve them.

The June 17, 1853, edition of the Richmond Daily Inquirer carried the following advertisement: "For Hire,

PLANTATION SHOWS

either by day, month or year, the services of one George Walker, the best leader of a band in all middle and eastern Virginia." Toler and Cook, slave brokers, were to be paid Walker's fees unless previously arranged. This probably made Toler and Cook the first theatrical agents.

Another black performer who proved to be a money-making proposition for his master was Solomon Northrup. In his published memoirs, speaking of his life on a Louisiana plantation, Northrup wrote: "My master often received letters, sometimes from a distance of ten miles, requesting him to send me to play at a ball or festival for the whites. He received his compensation, but usually I also returned with many picayunes jingling in my pockets."

Blind Tom, among the most noted of the slave musicians, was a child prodigy from Georgia. His master and booker was one Colonel Bethune. Being an extremely talented pianist and composer, Tom was able to continue his concert career long after the Emancipation.

The earliest record of slave entertainers goes back to the late eighteenth century, but it is certain that such performers were probably around as far back as the early seventeenth century, when the slaves were first dropped off at Jamestown.

The black entertainers found that performing paid off in more ways than just a visit to different plantations. Because of their elevated status, they were given better food and lodging and were treated preferentially. This, coupled with the coins they sometimes reaped after a particularly good performance, made entertaining profitable to them. So long as they entertained well, they didn't have to go out into the fields to work; they were special blacks.

The term black was not used, however. Instead, the slaves were called colored, Negro, nigger, darky, and nigra. And there was a definite hierarchy among them. Slaves who were the offspring of a master and a slave may have been looked down upon by the whites, but they, in turn, looked down on slaves with two black parents. With

PLANTATION SHOWS

the intermingling and color status came the half-black mulatto, the one-eighth-black octoroon, and the coffee-colored blacks, each with a place in the hierarchy and each with his or her own set of problems. It was not at all unusual to see a red-headed, brown-skinned pickaninny on the plantation grounds. Sometimes these children were picked to be the playmates of the master's white children. When they grew older, they were given the choice jobs inside the house and became the "house nigras." The progeny of two slaves most often worked in the fields and were called "field nigras."

The house slaves eventually became very close to their masters, to the point of becoming their counterparts. They waited on their owners, watched over them, and quickly developed all their mannerisms. They were so practiced, they became whites in black skin. In cases of light-colored blacks, some were so light-skinned they could pass for white—and did so as soon as they got a chance to run away. Others, sent away to school by fond masters, never came back.

Most of these runaways used the talents they had learned on the plantation to survive. They performed where they could, usually in medicine shows. Doing what they knew best, they blacked up and became blackface comedians, lampooning field slaves by dancing and clowning and acting the nigger. It was their only means of survival. And survive they did. The black entertainers started a whole new brand of entertainment in America—the minstrel show.

HARVEY'S GREATER MINSTRELS'

MINSTREL
SHOWS

MINSTREL SHOWS

Black slaves may have been the inspiration for minstrel shows, but it took white entertainers to bring them first to the American public and then to the world. As this country's initial original art form, a totally unique American phenomenon, minstrelsy stood out as something definitely special. It took the country by storm and its popularity quickly spread across the Atlantic. By the mid-1840s, minstrel shows were the hottest form of entertainment going.

No one is quite sure exactly when white men first put burnt cork on their faces and pranced out onstage giving their imitation of blacks. Who the first blackface entertainer was is also unknown. But as early as the 1820s there were white men promoting themselves as "Ethiopian delineators," as they called themselves back then, who purported to do authentic black songs, dances, and jokes, which they claimed to have borrowed from the blacks. At that time, many entertainers were dipping into American folklore to bring the public characterizations of real people. While some imitated the New Englander, calling him "the Yankee," others presented "the Frontiersman" by impersonating Davy Crockett. Still others toured the country in blackface. These performers traveled with circuses, entertained between the acts of a play, and even worked Barnum's Museum. They went onstage as single acts and did a set routine.

These performers all had one thing in common: they all stressed the authenticity of their portrayals, assuring the public that what they said and did actually was the way the type of people they were imitating really did speak, act, dance, and sing. While the broadening of their characters to the point of caricature for comedic purposes did little harm to New Englanders and frontiersmen as a whole, it did adversely affect blacks for well over 100 years. Their inaccuracy was to cause the unfair and incorrect stereotyping of an entire race. It is doubtful that the Ethiopian delineators did so maliciously; they were merely actors,

MINSTREL SHOWS

singers, and comedians who wanted to please their audiences more than they wanted to portray the truth. If the blacks were to suffer from these white men's caricature of them, the opportunistic performers were unaware of it. They were only interested in the sudden interest taken in the black characterizations they were presenting.

In 1828 Thomas Dotsmore Rice, who went by the stage name of Danny Rice, was casting about for something new to add to his act. He was an actor, a song-and-dance man, a traveling minstrel who often performed in blackface. But he needed something different to set him apart from the others, something original. While he was wandering through the South, he happened across a crippled black stablehand who was amusing himself with a little song and dance as he went about his work. As soon as Rice saw the stableman's pathetically comic dance and heard his catchy song, he knew he was seeing just what he had been looking for. After watching the cripple hop and jump and do his little dance step several times, Rice had memorized both the lyrics of the song and the pattern of the dance. He even went so far as to buy the crippled stablehand's raggedy clothes off his back so he could have as authentic an act as possible.

After adding several topical lines of lyrics to the original and upping the tempo to a much faster beat, Danny Rice was ready to present his characterization. He went out onstage, dancing and singing the stablehand's song:

Wheel about, turn about, and do jus' so,
And every time I wheel about, I jump Jim Crow.

"Jump Jim Crow" caught on from the moment it was presented to the public. Everyone wanted to learn how to do the dance. They all wanted to hop around and twist that funny way. Rice became known as Jim Crow Rice, and he was soon the toast of New York City and London.

MINSTREL SHOWS

Adding to his act little by little, Rice stretched that hobbled black stablehand's twisted comic jig into a twenty-year career. He never progressed much past the Jim Crow stage, but with such wide public acceptance, he didn't really need to. Whenever he wanted another caricature, he would go to the source: the South. He developed other characters: a town dandy, a flatboatman, a plantation fieldhand; then he added John Jefferson III, a little white boy, to his act.

Rice would stride onstage carrying a large gunny sack that was full and heavy. Putting the sack down, he would start to dance. On a given cue, little John, in full blackface, would pop out of the sack and begin to dance behind Rice, doing the shadow dance that was to be copied many years later by Ted Lewis and his shadow, Paul White. Rice's shadow dance was not all that was copied from him. Two more blackface performers, Billy Whitlock and Ben Cotton, who also dipped into the reservoir of black talent by studying the antics of black entertainers, jumped on the Jim Crow bandwagon and gained quite good reputations as fine Ethiopian delineators.

Everyone seemed to be satirizing the slaves. It was not only fashionable to do so, it was also very profitable, since the public was eating it up. Another performer who stole from Rice was Dan Emmett. Emmett was no piker—he stole Rice's entire act, lock, stock, and jig. A few years later, Emmett found himself stranded and unemployed in New York City. When he bumped into Billy Whitlock and two other blackface entertainers who were also out of work, he suggested they combine forces and put on a four-man, all-blackface show. They called themselves the Virginia Minstrels, since Virginia was the most popular state in the South, and they borrowed Minstrel from a very popular group of touring Europeans whose act had "minstrel" in its name.

Thus, in 1843, the first blackface minstrel show in the world, the Virginia Minstrels, opened in New York City.

MINSTREL SHOWS

They were not only an overnight smash, they became a fad that lasted. Unwittingly, they had created a demand for this uniquely American art form that was to continue for over 80 years. The public was clamoring for more; they just couldn't get enough. Other minstrel shows began to pop up all over the country: the Virginia Serenaders, the Kentucky Minstrels, the Ethiopian Minstrels, the San Francisco Minstrels, and many more. All the minstrel shows that followed the original had this element in common: they contained only white male performers who appeared in blackface.

Stages were flooded with one minstrel show after another, all using songs, dances, and jokes taken straight from the black slaves. These white entertainers literally made millions of dollars from stealing the black people's material; yet the black people, who were barred from most theaters and segregated in others, were not allowed to see the minstrel shows. And they definitely were banned from performing in them. So while the blacks furnished the white entertainers with their inspiration and most of their material, they reaped no rewards in the way of either credit or money. Of course, they would not have wanted to take credit for the farcical manner in which their impersonators portrayed them.

The minstrels copied the jigs and jubas of the black fieldhands and the cakewalk of the house servants. They also borrowed the stick dance and switched it to their own comedy routines. A white man, made up and dressed to look like an extremely fragile elderly plantation slave would hobble onstage to do the stick dance. After taking the audience in with his arthritic hobble, the "old man" would not only jump over the stick, he would do a complete backflip. Then he would proceed to do cartwheels and frantic dancing in total contrast with his apparent advanced age. Audiences went wild.

The cakewalk was patterned after dance competitions the house slaves would hold in which they would dress up

in their owners' cast-off clothes and strut and prance with a cake as the first prize. The dance was a combination strut and high kick. The juba, a completely original slave dance brought over from Africa and combined from the dances of many different tribes, is a very complex combination of hand-clapping, knee- and thigh- and shoulder-slapping done to a precise rhythmical pattern of steps. Its intricacy fascinated even the writers of the era. Such renowned poets as Edgar Allen Poe and Sidney Lanier were quick to tap the potential use of the varied beats for the metre to their verses. One of Poe's friends commented: "There are no such rhythms as this in Greek poetry, nor, in fact, in any other nation under the sun." Of the fascinating rhythmic body-slapping, foot-stomping, and singing of the juba, Lanier wrote: "Here music is in its rudest form consisting of rhythm alone, the most curious noise, yet in such perfect order it furnishes music to dance by. I've never seen it equalled in my life."

The most famous and talented juba dancer of all time was William Henry Lane, the only black entertainer in minstrelsy until the Civil War. His stage name was Juba, and he is recognized by historians as the father of tap dancing. Combining the regular Irish jig with the rhythmic patterns of the Afro-American juba dance, he created the dance form that has lasted for nearly 140 years and is just now enjoying a resurgence.

Juba's dancing abilities caught on, and by 1845 he was being touted as the greatest dancer ever. Juba's popularity not only swept this country, but it spilled over to Great Britain. In London, he was a sensation. The British were amazed at his dexterity, sense of rhythm, and grace. He beat his feet on the stage as no other dancer had ever done before and caused quite a stir among patrons and critics alike. Charles Dickens became one of his fans and found himself at a total loss for words to describe Juba's wondrous feats.

Unfortunately, although he created America's first and most lasting original dance, which had a permanent effect

MINSTREL SHOWS

on all dancers since, he is rarely given credit for it. It is possible that this is because his young life was tragically cut short and his incredible accomplishments spanned only a fourteen-year period, less than ten of which were spent in this country. In 1848 Juba had taken England by storm as a member of the Ethiopian Serenaders; he died in 1852, having just turned twenty-seven.

The first minstrel shows were slightly ragged around the edges, since all the entertainers were actually used to performing as single acts and couldn't quite make the transition to cohesiveness. As time passed and the minstrels became more practiced in their new format, the minstrel show began to take its final form. The show presented a minimum of fifteen white men all made up in blackface. Their eyes were exaggeratedly large by adding clown-white makeup around them; their mouths were also enlarged to give the impression of huge lips; their faces were totally covered with black soot from a burnt cork; their heads were covered with outsized black wooly wigs to accentuate the black people's hair; and their shoes were huge and floppy, to emphasize the stereotype of big feet.

The show was cut into three parts: the musical numbers, plus jokes and riddles; the variety section; and a plantation skit. Heading up the show were its three stars: Mr. Interlocutor, Mr. Bones, and Mr. Tambo. The interlocutor, dressed beautifully and acting with great pomposity, was the master of ceremonies, onstage director of the show, and brunt of all the jokes; he sat in the center of the semicircle of minstrels. On either end were the endmen, Mr. Bones and Mr. Tambo, who were dressed as gaudily as possible and who acted foolishly. Mr. Bones played the clacker bones, and Mr. Tambo played the tambourine; both were the comedians of the show whose quick repartee with the interlocutor usually ripped the shows wide open with laughter.

The endmen were always active, always in motion even when not talking. Cocking their heads to one side, jumping up and down, standing on their heads, howling, rolling

MINSTREL SHOWS

their eyes, laughing at nothing, they became the basis for American comic antics, and their bits became the standard for American humor. The endmen created the basic jokes that are still with us today, such as why the chicken crossed the road and why firemen wear red suspenders. They could make or break a show, and many theaters would not book in a minstrel show unless assured that the endmen were very good, because their audiences would stand for nothing less than the best. The public obviously came to see and hear the endmen, although the musical and variety numbers were important. Without good endmen, though, the show was considered wanting.

The rest of the minstrels played banjos, shook tambourines, and sang vocal solos—there was always one extremely high-pitched tenor and one extremely deep-voiced bass in every show.

In the first segment of the minstrel show, the entire troupe would come marching onstage singing some rousing song. They would file into a semicircle and stand in front of the seats provided for them and wait, singing, or they would already be onstage when the curtain went up, and they would begin shaking their tambourines and other instruments as they came into view. Then Mr. Interlocutor would command: "Gentlemen, be seated!" and the show would begin, loudly and with great gusto. The first part of the show was comprised of single and group songs and dances, lively choruses, banjo solos, sentimental ballads, comedy songs, and rapid-fire jokes and gags between the endmen and the interlocutor. There was never a dull moment, never a pause in the festivities. The comedy would usually proceed as follows:

> MR. BONES: Mr. Interlocutor, sir!
> INTERLOCUTOR: Yes, Mr. Bones?
> MR. BONES: Mr. Interlocutor, sir. Does us black folks go to hebbin? Does we go through dem golden gates?

MINSTREL SHOWS

INTERLOCUTOR: Mr. Bones, you know the golden gates is for white folks.

MR. TAMBO: Well, who's gonna be dere to open dem gates for you white folks?

The bones and tambourines would join in with the laughter. The act ended with an upbeat musical finale for the entire troupe and then the traditional walkaround just before the first intermission.

In the second part, which was performed in front of the drop curtain so the third-act scenery could be set up during the show, was called the olio and each man got a chance to entertain. The olio was a variety show and was the basis of what was later to become vaudeville when the other two sections of the minstrel show were dropped. During this part, the minstrels did their specialty acts, from playing the comb to acrobatics to playing spoons to juggling.

The comedy spot of the second act was usually the stump speaker, which was the minstrels' version of the story monologue. A comic would get up and give a speech, usually political in nature, that would be full of malapropisms and non-sequiturs. Lecturing on some topic or other, the stump speaker would unintelligibly bluster his way through one nonsensical phrase after another, presumably showing how foolish blacks could sound when trying to speak like the white man. (Professor Irwin Corey was the "stump speaker" of our day.) They also lampooned the subject matter, talking on women's rights, education, temperance, and other issues of the day with a false dignity that mocked the serious speechmakers. Although they brought subjects to the audiences' attention, they played it strictly for laughs.

At the end of the olio, the performers would take turns moving to front and centerstage to do a reprise of their act and then dance themselves breathless in a splashy finish.

MINSTREL SHOWS

Before the Civil War, the third act was always a plantation skit, and during and after the war, sometimes a topical skit. In it, a man was dressed up as a mammy in a big bustle, a woolly wig with a large red bandana wrapped around it, swishing taffeta skirts, and huge lips painted blood red.

From the 1840s through the late 1850s, with the exception of William Henry "Juba" Lane, no blacks set foot onstage as minstrels. They found other outlets, performing in traveling medicine shows and working carnivals. They acted as clowns to draw crowds of people to the medicine shows and carnivals, keeping them laughing while the barker tried to persuade them to buy admission to the carnival or buy a bottle of remedy. But with the signing of the Emancipation Proclamation in 1863, the status of the blacks was changed. It was their ticket to freedom, and for the black comics, it was a ticket onstage the theaters that had been closed to them before. Now they were able to work as regular comedians rather than merely as clowns.

BLACK MINSTREL
SHOWS

BLACK MINSTRELS

When the Civil War broke out, there was a large number of black entertainers in the North who joined the Union Army. In some cases, these early black performers put on shows for their troops, becoming a sort of forerunner of the USO.

Directly after the war, black minstrel shows began to spring up all over the country. Black entertainers began to show people that they could outclown, outjig, outshout, outdance, outcoon, and outdraw any and all white impersonators. Why not? They were the real thing. This they emphasized in their advertisements and in their billing. One such black minstrel show, Brooker and Clayton's Georgia Minstrels, proclaimed in 1865–66 that they were "The Only Simon Pure Negro Troupe in the World." They were trying to compete with the white minstrels, who had a strong foothold in American theater, and they had to prove themselves better than the whites if they were to win over the audiences.

The first all-black minstrel show was organized by Lew Johnson. His Plantation Company started in 1864 and brought a naturalness to the minstrel shows that had been lacking. To emphasize the distinction between the black and the white minstrel shows, black minstrels left off the burnt cork so the audiences could see their complexions' natural shades of brown. All but the endmen, who kept the comedy masks of the blackface comedian.

In 1865 another company of black minstrels was put together by Charles Hicks, himself a black. This show became so popular that it was soon taken over by Charles Callender, a white manager. With its new manager, the show became even more lucrative than before, touring the entire country for several years. In the 1870s, J. H. Haverly, widely considered the P. T. Barnum of minstrelsy, took the show over and took it abroad. Starring as the comedian was black comic Billy Kersands, whose mouth was so large he could easily fit a saucer or several golf balls into it. He would tell people, "If de Lo'd wanted my mouff to be bigger, He'd have to move mah ears."

BLACK MINSTRELS

Some of the others who formed very successful and flourishing black minstrel shows were Richards and Pringle, Hicks and Sawyer, and McCabe and Young. In 1883 Primrose and West really broke ground by organizing America's first racially mixed company, The Forty Whites and Thirty Blacks.

Early black minstrel stars included Wallace King, the marvelous falsetto singer who was billed as "The Man with the Child Voice"; Charles Cruso, a very funny monologist; and the "Two Bohee Brothers," who danced the soft-shoe while playing their banjos.

Black entertainers became well-seasoned travelers, playing throughout the United States, Canada, the South Pacific, and Europe. Some troupes were so fancy they had their own railway cars; others were so scraggly they barely made ends meet. They played for whites and blacks, in urban areas and rural, big cities and tiny western towns, in fancy theaters and rundown barns, for the rich and the poor, before farmhands and royalty. Many even owned their own shows and became great stars.

Unfortunately, these black entertainers were forced to play out the role set for them by the white men; they had to do caricatures of themselves. Besides suffering the indignity of acting the nigger, they faced frightening incidents ranging from hateful stares to lynchings. They were not welcome in many of the theaters they played as anything but performers—they couldn't set foot inside the house to watch a show; they had to be the show. They were still segregated.

Despite all the problems facing the blacks at the time, thousands of them jumped at the chance to be minstrels. After all, being a minstrel was one of the few ways open for black entertainers of the nineteenth century; there was almost no place else to play. So, while most blacks were switching from slavery to serfdom, the entertainers found a means of becoming somebody.

Black minstrels treasured the praise they received from white critics, but their greatest satisfaction came from

pleasing their black fans. It was not just little children who worshipped them, but lovely young ladies, too. The black women fairly swooned at the entertainers' fancy clothes and swaggering step. Right from the start, the black minstrel shows fared very well in black neighborhoods. They drew blacks to the theaters in droves. Some theater managers actually broke their segregation policies by accommodating all the black people who wanted tickets to their shows.

It was only in black communities and sections of town that the black entertainers really felt at home and could enjoy the benefits of being somebody. They had no trouble finding places to stay or admiring fans to speak with. Another plus, at least when they were among other black people: they could act like themselves and not the caricatures they were forced to portray. Rarely were they permitted to show what they were really like while onstage. It was still a white man's world.

The myth that "all blacks have rhythm" is an enduring fallacy. Contrary to the racial stereotype of blacks being born musicians and natural entertainers, people of all races are genetically talented or untalented. Once given the opportunity, however, a large number of blacks excelled in show business, primarily because their Afro-American heritage and experiences had prepared them well for it. While the blacks may have legally had their freedom, their civil, economic, and political rights were completely denied them in the nineteenth century. Not too much had changed with Emancipation. In their religion and music, however, they found outlets for their otherwise pentup emotions and energies. Over the years they created a distinctive new culture, blending European and African arts into Afro-American ones, such as their spirituals, jazz, and dance forms. Blacks were drawn to show business as one of the few places open for advancement for their people.

BLACK MINSTRELS

Without realizing it, black minstrels contributed to America's racial mythology of the blacks. By stressing in their publicity that they were untutored plantation blacks, while trying to compete with the already established white minstrels, they gave the white public the impression that all black minstrels were naturally spontaneously talented people on exhibit, rather than artfully skilled pros who were executing predetermined entertainment. This image of black performers lived on long after minstrelsy died out. The whites actually believed they were seeing blacks doing what came naturally, and the blacks, trying to outstrip the white minstrels, didn't help any when they stressed their authenticity as true blacks and claimed close ties with actual slaves. Some blacks, to further emphasize the distinction, called their shows "Coon Show" and "Jig Show." It may have helped their business, but it certainly didn't make the path any less bumpy for generations to come.

"All the best black talent of that generation came down the same drain," commented W. C. Handy, father of the blues, who started his career in minstrelsy. Handy pointed out that the entertainers for generations ahead all had their roots in the minstrel show, from the composer to the singer to the musician to the comedian and the stage performer.

James Bland, composer of "Carry Me Back to Old Virginny," "In the Evening by the Moonlight," and "Dem Golden Slippers," as well as hundreds of other songs, was the most prolific, well-known, and influential black composer to come out of the minstrelsy. Born of free black parents on Long Island, Bland went to Howard University, where he trained as a composer and arranger. As a child he had been given a banjo and had made up music on it. While still in his teens, he got up the nerve to go backstage at the Ford Theatre in Washington one night to play some of his songs for the famous white minstrel George Primrose. The performer was so taken by Bland's melodies that

he brought him to the attention of the white manager of Haverly's all-black minstrel show. The college-educated musician was signed and billed as "the world's greatest minstrel man." He sailed to London with the show and became an overnight success; the handsome young singer was just what the British public had been waiting for. It wasn't long before his songs were being sung in all the music halls.

Bland may have had a genius for composing, but he won his acclaim from a white public who dearly loved his caricatures of the blacks. They praised him by calling him the black Stephen Foster, since his songs were primarily of blacks who were gaudily dressed, of old blacks who adored living with their white folks, of self-indulgent and highly religious church-going blacks, and cocky but stupid northern blacks with the stereotyped big feet and mouths hanging open. Bland's work is a testament to the price paid by the blacks if they were to succeed in a white man's world.

As the times changed, the popular songs began to combine ragtime with lyrics that put the blacks down with renewed fervor. Besides sustaining the stereotype of blacks as chicken-munching clowns, these new "coon songs" not only portrayed the exaggerated facial features already caricatured, they also added a new image: the black as a razor-packing man of violence. These newest songs almost made the slave stereotypes acceptable by comparison.

By the turn of the century, the latest coon songs began to contain even more tasteless and objectionable lyrics and titles. Whites went crazy over such songs as "He's Just a Little Nigger, But He's Mine, All Mine," "Coon, Coon, How I Wish My Color Would Change," and "You May Be a Hawaiian on Broadway, But You're Just Another Nigger to Me." In describing what a coon flag looked like, someone claimed it was made of red cloth with a possum rampant over a crossed pork chop and ham bone, with a flying

Two Typical Black Minstrels

chicken holding a banjo in one claw and a pair of dice in the other.

The nineteenth-century black entertainers who pioneered in show business had to struggle against heavy odds to make careers for themselves and to modify or break free of the minstrel stereotypes and restrictions. They were among the most creative and gifted entertainers in America, and they laid the groundwork that has endured for blacks in show biz. The story of blacks in entertainment, like the broader story of blacks in America, is a bittersweet blend of triumph and joy mixed well with tragedy and tears.

One of those entertainers who struggled against overwhelming odds was Sam Lucas, who became one of the minstrel greats. Although he was a serious actor, he was forced to play the clown in the minstrelsy, starring in Haverly's Colored Minstrels when it went to London in 1865. A brilliant performer and a very proud man who exhibited an independence not usually seen in entertainers of his day, Lucas made up his mind that he was going to break free of the limits set on black entertainers. His efforts are witness to the restrictions put on those frustrated pioneers.

Born in 1850, the son of Ohio free blacks, Lucas became a minstrel while still in his teens. Inside of four years he had reached the pinnacle of minstrelsy, starring as a singer, composer, and character actor specializing in portraying old men. When he was only twenty-five, he left minstrelsy and became the serious actor he had always wanted to be. He was cast in an operatic drama, Out of Bondage, which was the predecessor of the black musical. It starred black singers Anna and Emma Hyer, but it lacked public backing. Without an audience, it soon folded, forcing Lucas to return to being a minstrel just when he was about to break fresh ground.

In 1878 Lucas became the first black man to be cast in the title role of a serious adaptation of Uncle Tom's Cabin.

BLACK MINSTRELS

Heretofore the role had always been considered by white producers to be too demanding for a black man, whom they felt wouldn't be able to learn all the lines and perform them properly. Lucas got his chance when the managers of a dying comedy troupe decided to hype business by offering the authentic version of the play, with a real black man playing Tom. The managers sent for Lucas, asking him to bring his diamonds along just in case.

With a badly miscast cast, including an obese Little Eva, the troupe soon found themselves stranded on the road. This is where Lucas's diamonds came in—he had to pawn them to get enough money to pay their way back to the nearest big city. Back to the minstrelsy went a sadder but wiser Sam Lucas.

Although Lucas had the talent and the know-how to take over and run his own minstrel show, his interests were elsewhere and he passed the opportunities by. As a star of the first magnitude, he played in all the top companies; as a composer he published a great number of songs, only one of which has endured: "Grandfather's Clock."

Unlike Bland, who knuckled under to white pressure, Lucas did all he could to play down the black stereotypes. The blacks in his songs loved freedom, not the white folks: "I nebber shall forget, no nebber, de day I was sot free," sang one of his song's characters. In another, he praised Emancipation Day as the "happiest day de colored man e'er knew."

By the 1890s, Lucas got the chance that he had been looking for to break real ground for his people. Just as soon as blacks were allowed to play white vaudeville, Lucas and his wife were booked onto the prestigious Loew circuit, which was shaking free the shackles of the minstrel show format. He was making headway. With his career in show business now spanning nearly a half-century, Lucas again recorded another first as the first black man to star in a movie. In 1915 he was cast in the title role of <u>Uncle Tom's Cabin</u>. Shortly after finishing the picture in 1916,

BLACK MINSTRELS

Sam Lucas died. His achievements in show business prompted black civil rights leader James Weldon Johnson, himself a poet and songwriter, to give Lucas the well-earned title of "The Grand Old Man of the Negro Stage."

In the 1890s, interest in plantation blacks was dwindling rapidly. So, although there were a few lingering minstrel troupes still on the boards, and southern musicals such as The South Before the War and In Old Kentucky still portrayed the minstrel-type darkies, drastic changes in the black entertainment marketplace were going on. The whites' taste in black entertainment had changed very little; they still saw blacks as gamboling innocents, eternally youthful until elderly. They merely switched the scene from the South to the North, adjusting to the appropriate dances and musical instruments. Hoedowns and banjos were out; city struts and piano and ragtime were in.

Ragtime music was a pastiche of black American rhythms and white American tunes, and the new black musicals embraced a combination of the best of minstrel shows, ragtime, black American dances, vaudeville, and musical comedy. Although they still held the blacks to their stereotypes, the black musicals allowed the entertainers to show more of their talents and exhibit their versatility. Thus able to let the public know what they could really do, they climbed higher and higher on the ladder of Broadway success and stardom.

The Creole Show, the first black show to drop the straight minstrelsy format, opened in Boston in 1890, featuring, for the first time on any stage, sixteen beautiful black chorus girls. Although the show kept its three-part format and semicircle, it emphasized the women's bodies, the songs of the day, and topical humor. The plantation was definitely out. The show was such a smash hit that it ran for years on the road. In 1891 the original cast moved to Chicago and opened in Sam T. Jack's Opera House. It had a five-year run there and played during the Chicago World's Fair.

BLACK MINSTRELS

In 1895 the black advance man for <u>The Creole Show</u>, Jack Isham, organized and produced another show that dumped even more of the minstrel atmosphere, <u>The Octoroons</u>. It, too, became a hit just as had its predecessor at the Opera House.

A third black stage show, <u>In Oriental America</u>, kept very little of the minstrelsy and put the spotlight on the lovely women, variety acts, and jazzy ragtime rhythms. This show eliminated the old traditional walkaround. And it replaced the stump speaker closing with tenors Sydney Woodward and J. Rosamond Johnson, and Inez Clough doing an operatic medley. Taking tradition-breaking a step further, the show played at the Palmer Theatre, which later became Wallack's, rather than the usual burlesque house.

The greatest departure of the century from the minstrel show thus far was <u>A Trip to Coontown</u>, which university-educated Bob Cole wrote, directed, and produced in 1898. It offered the audience a plot and a continuity of characters, and it was another landmark: it was the first complete musical to be written, produced, directed, and performed by blacks. It opened in April 1898 in New York's Third Avenue Theatre and starred Sam Lucas and Jesse Shipp, who later wrote for Williams and Walker.

Will Marion Cook, graduate of Oberlin Conservatory and the National Conservatory of Music in New York, wrote a musical sketch in 1898, <u>Clorindy</u>. The show was an even larger departure from traditional minstrel shows than its predecessors in that it contained ragtime rhythms, an overpowering chorale, showy dancers, and such stars as ragtime composer and performer Ernest Hogan, "the Unbleached American."

Cook took another giant step for black entertainers when he tried to get his show booked into the Casino Theatre roof garden in New York. Trying for months to talk Edward E. Rice, the theater's manager, into granting his company an audition, Cook was repeatedly refused. For over a month he nearly camped out in Rice's office, but to

no avail. Finally, out of desperation, Cook took his well-rehearsed cast of twenty-six to an open audition. He had prepared a little surprise for Rice: when the manager entered the audition room, the entire cast broke into a rousing chorale number, "Darktown Is Out Tonight." Rice was swept up by the stirringly rhythmic beat and he booked the show into his theater and it was a smash.

At last blacks were on Broadway—or, technically, above it in the roof garden. Cook prematurely and enthusiastically announced: "Gone·was the uff-dah of the minstrel! Gone the Massa Linkum stuff! We were artists and we were going a long, long way." Cook was right in one respect, his performers definitely were artists who had come a long way. But they were still chained to the stereotype and hampered by discrimination.

Sadly, while both Bob Cole and Will Cook had such scholarly musical backgrounds, they were never permitted to put their tutored talents to the test by giving them free rein. Both composers realized they had to eat, and in order to do so, they were forced to write the coon songs and stereotyped sketches that were the white man's view of blacks. So their players strutted the cakewalk and sang such songs as "Who Dat Say Chicken in Dis Crowd?" and "Hottest Coon in Dixie."

Although blacks were "on Broadway," it was just in Clorindy, an all-black rooftop sketch, not a full-blown Broadway musical. After its summer booking, the show left town for a tour of the East. Ernest Hogan took the opportunity to switch to another show, and he was replaced by the up-and-coming comedy team of Bert Williams and George Walker, who took the show to Washington, D.C., Boston, Philadelphia, and Cincinnati. It may have been a good show, but the "Senegambian Carnival," as they were called, just couldn't make it on the road. The show finally folded, leaving Williams and Walker at liberty. Their time was yet to come.

BLACK MINSTRELS

The Creole Show, The Octoroons, and In Oriental America had several very important common bonds, besides being breakthroughs for trying to shed the minstrel bonds: all three shows presented beautiful black women in gorgeous costumes; all three permitted the women to achieve principal roles besides being in the chorus line; and the shows all hired trained black musicians and composers, who added a new dimension to their shows.

J. Rosamond Johnson, of In Oriental America, was more than just a tenor; he was a bright young composer who wrote many songs for the show, as well as arias. Johnson, whose brother was poet James Weldon Johnson, often collaborated with his brother on compositions. Together the brothers composed such lasting songs as "Under the Bamboo Tree," "My Castle on the Nile," "Since You Went Away," and "The Maiden with the Dreamy Eyes." In collaboration with Bob Cole, they wrote "Lazy Moon," and "Congo Love Song." J. Rosamond Johnson later wrote several of his own black musicals, including Shoo-Fly Regiment and Red Moon, in which he treated the audience to his lilting tenor renditions of his own songs. It wasn't long before producers realized what a goldmine they had in this literally untapped talent and took advantage of it. All these gifted composers were now beginning to receive a bit of the recognition they deserved.

The demise of the traditional minstrel show was at hand, and with the white producers' discovery of the rich talents of the well-trained black musicians and performers, black show business was coming into its own. The blacks were now getting their rewards through recognition. Such enormous talents as Bob Cole, Sam Lucas, Will Marion Cook, J. Rosamond Johnson, and Paul Lawrence Dunbar helped black artists forge ahead and climb out of their ruts.

While the musicians were able to let their abilities blossom and grow unfettered with the end of the minstrelsy,

BLACK MINSTRELS

the black entertainer was a different story. Most comedians were mulattos or octoroons, having been the offspring of some master's man. These light-skinned, coffee-colored comedians blacked their faces to keep themselves as blacks. They traded heavily on slave humor long into Reconstruction, and the specter of its slave-master relationship was to leave its mark on the following generation of black comedians.

Show business had been a haven for the black comedians, a refuge from slavery, then from lack of identity and sense of achievement. Now the comedians no longer had to prostitute their own race to make their name. Burlesquing their own people was not necessary; they could make it just as big by merely being themselves. They were on an equal footing professionally with the white performer, playing many of the same houses as the whites. And their new comedy routines were to set the pattern for comics to come. But with all this acceptance and renown, black entertainers still could not shake the bonds of prejudice and segregation that dogged their steps up the ladder of success.

HARLEM—1900

HARLEM—1900

With the emerging black entertainer's continued success, white America became increasingly alarmed and felt more and more threatened. A large New York suburb, Harlem, that had been planned and designated for wealthy whites was now fast becoming a black ghetto. Black theaters and shows were flourishing there. This only added fuel to the already raging fire of racial tension. One critic of the day was quick to point out: "If they were content to be 'darkies' with an exhibition of the rhythmic charm which made the 'darky' fascinating, one might endure them," but, he cried, "they do white sketch acts." This twentieth-century spokesman for the whites of that day was voicing what everyone else was thinking: blacks were beginning to forget their "place" and were stepping on white toes in the process.

The terror felt by some whites witnessing the coming of age of the childlike "darkies" was further expressed by another critic at the turn of the century, who saw the blacks' meteoric rise in show business as a dark omen, foreshadowing "the growing commonness of the inter-mingling of the races which cannot but end in results that will be extremely discussed in medical publications." Fear of black infiltration and permutation of their race was based on the blacks' newfound recognition and discontent with holding down inferior jobs.

Northern whites, seeing a threat to their own job stability and the possible loss of their women, railed against the overwhelming migration of southern blacks. The whites had nothing against black entertainers, but they saw the breaking away from the stereotype as just another step closer to infringing on their traditional ways. The blacks were flooding into the North as fast as industrial job opportunities opened up to accommodate them. And Jack Johnson, the black fighter who became boxing's heavyweight champion of the world in 1908 was no help to the cause; all whites could see was that this powerful black man made a living from beating up white men and used his winnings to

HARLEM—1900

keep white mistresses. What more tangible threat could there be?

White enthusiasm had changed with the evolving black entertainers' freedom. From 1898 to 1910 there had been a wholesale migration of blacks from all over—the South, the border states, the West Indies. And they had all headed for Harlem, the black utopia. Show business was booming, with the ranks of blacks doubling from 1890 through 1910. At the 1910 census, there were 3,098 black people listed in show business. It had been a good time for entertainers of both races, with theaters booming in the smallest towns and the biggest cities.

New York City was a mecca for both black and white performers, and such black greats as Bob Cole, Williams and Walker, and J. Rosamond Johnson were the toasts of the town. On first arriving in New York, southern blacks were able to forget the oppressive prejudice of the South and could freely strut down Broadway in style.

The climate soon changed, however, and the threatened whites were beginning to show their muscles again. After what they saw as a black takeover of Harlem, whites began shoving back. They started with the black entertainers and pushed them farther north—off Broadway and into Harlem. No longer welcome in white theaters, the blacks were forced to play only the Lincoln and Lafayette theaters. As further evidence of the white boycott, when Florenz Ziegfeld bought the finale of Darktown Follies, the black cast did not move downtown with it. Ziegfeld, bowing to the pressures of an enraged public, cast whites instead.

The threat finally turned to violence when a bloody race riot broke out in 1900 in New York City after a black criminal killed a white police officer. Mob violence resulted, with whites flooding into black areas and destroying whatever they could. As they went, they cried out: "Get Ernest Hogan," "Get Cole and Johnson," and "Get Williams and Walker." Having singled out the most famous black entertainers, they decided to take out their hostil-

ities on what they considered to be "uppity niggers." Hogan was so badly mauled by the rioters that he had to leave the show he was starring in; George Walker was more fortunate—he hid out in a dark celler until it was all over.

In 1903, when Williams and Walker opened on Broadway in their <u>In Dahomey</u>, everyone waited, sure there would be a recurrence of the earlier race riot, but none occurred. It was neither violence nor envy that cleared Broadway of its black entertainers; it was prejudice pure and simple. The moneymen and the producers, whose pocketbooks could be swayed by the white people's attitudes, helped exclude the blacks. But it didn't happen overnight; it was a slow process in which the year 1910 played a critical role. By then, Ernest Hogan, Bob Cole, and George Walker had all been struck by illness, leaving behind them no replacements as show producers and troupe managers to follow in their footsteps.

In 1910 Bert Williams put out the last light of hope for black shows on Broadway when he signed as the first black star to join the fabulous <u>Ziegfeld Follies</u>. Williams was the last black star whose brilliance could draw an audience and whose name could carry an all-black show. So, without its major producers, managers, and stars, black show business fell victim to white bias and shriveled up into a ghetto-oriented phenomenon for many years.

WILLIAMS & WALKER

WILLIAMS & WALKER

The careers of Bert Williams and George Walker closely followed the history of black entertainment in America. Their ups and downs, their struggling and accomplishment, their fame and pain were paralleled by the business itself. Their lives told the tale of all of black show business of the times.

George Walker was born in Kansas in 1873. By the time he was out of his teens, he was a seasoned veteran of the minstrel and medicine shows. Besides being a blackface comedian who used a tramp character as his act, he was also a very good dancer. He was twenty years old when he met Bert Williams while performing in San Francisco.

Williams was born in Antigua in the West Indies a year after Walker; however, his parents moved the family to Riverside, California, when Williams was eleven. While his father worked as a railroad conductor, Williams graduated from high school and was accepted at Stanford University. He was more interested in performing than in learning, however, so he left Stanford after just a semester or so. Attracted by the Barbary Coast saloons of nearby San Francisco, he studied piano while working there with a Hawaiian song-and-dance troupe. When he was offered a booking with a minstrel show that was going to tour northern California lumber camps, he jumped at the opportunity.

Having come from the West Indies, the slave dialect that he and the others were forced to use was difficult to master. As Williams put it, it was "as much a foreign dialect as that of Italian." But he learned it and made a living at it. He was earning a good seven dollars a week back in San Francisco when his path crossed Walker's. The two young men decided that their comedy was far enough apart to make a good team. Their two-man team lasted sixteen years and made a lot of history.

Their early days together were less than memorable. They played beatup variety houses in San Francisco from 1893 to 1894, unable to find any better places to play that

WILLIAMS & WALKER

would have them. Finally, to eat, they even went so far as to accept a job in the Golden Gate Park African Dahomean Village exhibit, dressing in animal skins and appearing as authentic savages from Africa.

Realizing that there were better things to do in show business than play savages, they headed for Chicago to try out for a new show they had heard about, The Octoroons. Their course was a bit circuitous, since they could not afford the luxury of going straight to Chicago. Without the necessary funds, they had to work their way there. Taking jobs with any and every medicine show, they did what most other performers were doing, acting as clowns for the hucksters on the wagons.

They made the mistake of going through Texas on their way to the Windy City. They were in the South, and southern whites didn't care much for "uppity niggers" who dressed too well for blacks. They had their clothes ripped off them and replaced with what the whites considered more fitting: gunny sacks. This episode was to scar Williams for life, since he was a very sensitive person who had always valued being accepted by both whites and blacks. Walker may have been angry, but he didn't let the incident get to him. His interests were in the black community, and he cared little what whites thought of him. Williams, on the other hand, wanted everyone's acceptance.

Finally arriving in Chicago after their many adventures on the road, they were hired right away to work in The Octoroons. They were also fired right away, lasting only one week in the show, after all the trouble they had gone through to get there. They soon learned that it would take more than just a common vaudeville act such as theirs to break into the big time. They had failed at their first chance, but they now knew what it would take to make it: a great deal of improvement.

Joining a small variety troupe, they toured the Midwest as "The Two Real Coons." To accentuate the differences between them, Walker added sparkle to his gaudily

dressed dandy characterization, while Williams increased the buffoonery of his Stepin Fetchit-type character. By putting on blackface, Williams added the final touch to his light skin that would heighten the humor.

Once in blackface, Williams found that a whole new world was his. Hiding behind a mask helped him to open up, as it had many an endman. As he recalled it: "Then I began to find myself. It was not until I was able to see myself as another person that my sense of humor developed." His comedic confidence grew when he wore the blackface makeup, and he was able to do and say things he would not normally have said and done. The whites dictated that his character be a fool, an ignorant, simple-minded jackass. But Williams couldn't do what was expected of him until he blacked up. Once hidden behind the cork, he, like so many other black comedians, could make a living doing something that was very distasteful to him.

After having worked out their roles very carefully to make sure there was enough difference between them, they brought their act to New York, the country's show business capital. They arrived in 1896, at the height of the "coon song" rage, and found that their gross "darky" and "dandy" characters were just what the public wanted. "The Two Real Coons" were a howling success and received a trial booking at Koster and Bial's Music Hall, one of New York's better variety houses. The critic from the New York Dramatic Mirror raved: "The dude member of the team does various funny walks." Continuing his lefthanded praise, he pointed out that "the common every-day Nigger has only to open his mouth to bring laughs."

Williams and Walker were indeed making it. They followed their first music hall booking with even bigger hits at Tony Pastor's Music Hall, Oscar Hammerstein's Olympia Roof Garden, and B. F. Keith's in Boston. They were on their way to stardom, but their manager felt that a national reputation was in order and might just do the trick; so the team joined an otherwise all-white vaudeville troupe that

WILLIAMS & WALKER

included McIntyre and Heath, two masters of the black-face. By the time Williams and Walker returned to New York in 1898, they had become proficient at both cake-walking and clowning.

Although the cakewalk had been included in minstrel shows since the early 1870s, the dance had reached epidemic proportions by the 1890s. Williams and Walker were surefire hits with their two coffee-colored cakewalking ladies on their arms. And while the dance had originally been a spoof on high society, now it was high society's turn to do the dance. Society pages were full of pictures of prominent New Yorkers strutting their stuff. To take advantage of this rage, the team ingeniously challenged William K. Vanderbilt to a cakewalking contest with fifty dollars in prize money and the title of world champion cakewalker at stake. Their clever ploy couldn't have brought them better publicity.

A great deal of the team's popularity was based on the fact that Walker was a marvelous dancer whose high-stepping kicks were awesome to watch, while Williams's pathetically humorous clowning attempts to dance made audiences feel less inadequate. The two men offered the public someone they could admire and someone they could laugh at. Theirs was a winning combination.

In 1899 they left the vaudeville music hall circuit to put together their own show called A Lucky Coon. Starring in this jumble of everything in the way of coonery, they toured the nation's second-rate theaters with such success that they soon became the equals of such top black stars as Bob Cole and Ernest Hogan.

By marrying Ada Overton, Walker added a beautiful and talented dancer to the show in feature billing. Now they were really making it big. They followed A Lucky Coon with two more hits: The Policy Players, about gambling, and Sons of Hams, which played for two years. With three smashes in a row, Williams and Walker decided to take some time off to plan the biggest and best black musical

to ever play anywhere; so in 1902 they sat down and planned In Dahomey. Walker wanted to emphasize the African side of Afro-American culture, but since neither member of the team knew anything about Africa, their show had little to do with it.

In Dahomey was about a bunch of nasty Boston businessmen who were plotting to colonize blacks to Africa. They send Rareback Pinkerton (Walker) to talk a senile but rich Floridian into financing the venture. Rareback tricks Shylock Homestead (Williams), a simple-minded Salvation Army drummer, into going with him to Florida to talk to the elderly moneyman into the plan. As it turns out, Shylock is the old man's long-lost heir. Rareback tries to get hold of the old man's fortune through Shylock and almost succeeds until Shylock unmasks Rareback and his conniving scheme.

The show became such a big hit with all its glorious production numbers that, after great reviews on the road, Williams and Walker brought their show to Broadway. After so many years of trying, they had finally made it to the very top. Williams was quoted as saying: "I used to be tempted to beg for a fifteen-dollar job in a chorus just for one week so as to say I'd been on Broadway once." But he wasn't in the chorus for a week; he was in his own smash hit for a long run. To add to the glory, in 1903 Theatre Magazine praised Williams to the skies, calling him "a vastly funnier man than any white comedian now on the stage."

For nearly all his career, Williams had played the dumb bumpkin who was constantly being duped by Walker. In his newest song for In Dahomey, "Jonah Man," the lyrics matched his life:

My luck started when I was born
Leas' so the old folks say.
Dat same hard luck's been my bes' frien'
To dis very day.

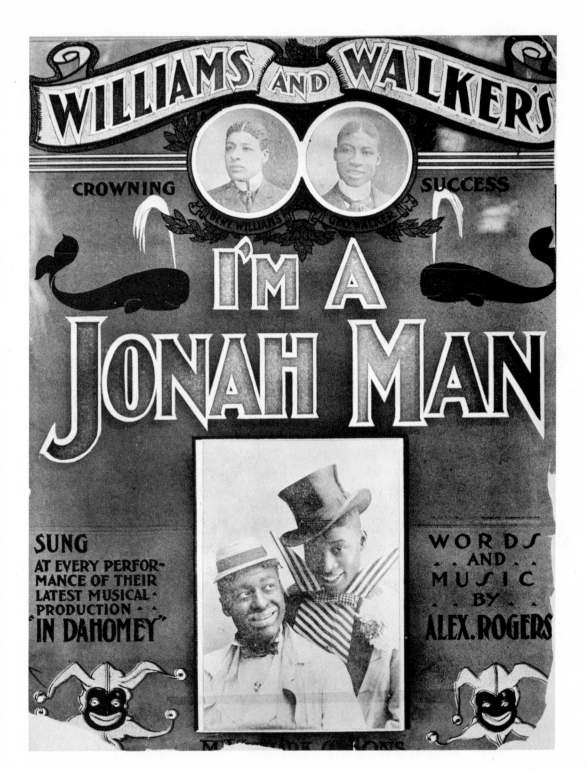

WILLIAMS & WALKER

With its tremendous run on Broadway over, Williams and Walker took their show to England, where they even played a command performance at Buckingham Palace.

Williams fell in love with the comparative lack of discrimination in Great Britain, finding he could talk with admirers on the street. He even joined an integrated Masonic Lodge. Just the opposite of Williams, Walker couldn't have cared less about white acceptance. He loved playing in America, as segregated as it was. The two men were obviously as different as night and day; Walker was nearly the same offstage as the character he played onstage. He thrived on publicity and never missed a chance to give the reporters something to talk about. He especially enjoyed the adoration of his black fans and always kept his eye out for admiring young women.

The team's next big hit was Abyssinia, which was written by Jesse Shipp, Alex Rogers, and Will Marion Cook. In February 1906, it opened at the Majestic Theatre. This show followed the same formula all their previous successes had: an exotic location, a well-rehearsed and boisterous chorus, a thrilling dance group, a plum of a role for Ada Overton Walker, a buffoonish hard-luck character for Bert, and a cocky dandy part for George. In Abyssinia, the plot finds Williams as a bedraggled American wandering through the magnificence of Black Abyssinia. Walker gives him some money to buy clothes, but he buys a camel instead. Then he is caught taking a precious vase and is about to be dragged before the emperor. The sentence for theft in Abyssinia is always having the guilty hand lopped off. Walker berates Williams for getting himself in such a pickle:

"Now you gone and done it. I bring you over here for you to get some culture and you go walking all through this culture, looking like some vulture. I even takes you swimming, half-hoping you'd drown, but the water takes one look at you and frowns, and it backs up to your knees. What you gonna do? You know the punishment for what

WILLIAMS & WALKER

you've done is to chop off your hand. What you gonna do with one hand and a nub? What you gonna do then?"

To which Williams replies:

"I'm gonna put a hook on it!"

In the next scene, Williams is brought before the emperor. Bert sings the touching song that sums up his role as the black man for whom nothing ever goes right. He is still remembered for his rendition of "Nobody":

I ain't never done nothin' to nobody,
And I ain't never got nothin' from nobody,
And until I get somethin' from somebody,
Sometime . . .
I ain't never gonna do nothin' for nobody,
No time.

Williams wrote the music to "Nobody," and Alex Rogers wrote the lyrics. Williams had such a hard time trying to remember the words that he finally wrote them down in his glove.

The team's biggest hit was their last: Banana Land, which opened in 1907. It was a fast-paced show with marvelous musical numbers by Will Marion Cook, Will Vodrey, and Alex Rogers. As always, Williams played a show-witted dude who was easily duped by fast-talking dandy Walker. This musical was more of a social commentary in which they satirized blacks moving into white neighborhoods and then using scare tactics to make money. Buying into an all-white area, they'd throw wild parties until the white neighbors would band together and buy the property back at inflated prices.

In Banana Land, Walker did his awe-inspiring strutting cakewalk with a line of beautiful girls and sang his famous song:

WILLIAMS & WALKER

Bon Bon Buddy, the Chocolate Drop
That's me, that's me,
Bon Bon Buddy, a Chocolate Drop
That's all I want to be.

Walker was onstage in Boston in 1909, doing this number after two successful years in New York and on the road, when he began to slur his words. The cast thought he was merely improvising; he wasn't. George Walker had suffered a stroke. He was rushed to a sanitarium in Kansas, where he remained until his death two years later.

For the first time in sixteen years, Williams was without a partner. With Walker's wife doing her husband's hit dance as a tribute to him, Williams tried to fulfill the team's advance bookings. But after just a month of it, Bert had to give up; he couldn't fill George's shoes as manager of the show. He was brilliant onstage, but offstage, as he said later, "I feel like a ship without a rudder." So Bert Williams went back to vaudeville, playing the best houses in the country. Until Walker's death, Williams shared his vaudeville salary with him. But in 1911, the world-famous team of Williams and Walker finally came to an end.

BERT WILLIAMS

BERT WILLIAMS

A year after George Walker's forced retirement, Bert Williams was signed to star in the Ziegfeld Follies of 1910. The show was a marvelous vehicle for the sad clown and, released from the "darky-dandy" format of the team, he could do more universal comedy. He played down-and-out boarders, porters, cab drivers, crap shooters, poker players. Any role that called for the downtrodden was Williams's meat. The pathos and dignity of his characters, along with his comedic genius, came through in the Follies. He made an even bigger impact on the audiences because he was surrounded by an otherwise all-white cast and gorgeous production numbers; thus he stood out in all his brilliance.

Well-known Chicago critic Ashton Stevens said of Williams, after having seen him in the Follies of 1910: "Bert Williams is the Mark Twain of his color. His was kindly, infectious humor, humor that made humans of us all." This was long overdue praise, the recognition he had waited so long for. Williams was quoted as commenting about his comedy: "The sight of other people in trouble is nearly always funny. Nearly all of my successful songs have been based on the idea that I am getting the worst of it. I am 'The Jonah Man,' the man who, even if it rained soup, would be found with a fork in his hand and no spoon in sight." Williams's method of wringing laughter from his audience was to let them know that although each character was in trouble, he was not being hurt even though he was "fielding flatirons with his head, carrying large bulldogs by the seat of his pants, and picking the bare bones of the chicken while his wife's relations eat the breast, and so forth."

Two of the greatest names in comedy, Eddie Cantor and W. C. Fields, played on the same bill with Williams, and both felt he was one of the top comedians of all time. Eddie Cantor went so far as to say of the man: "Whatever sense of timing I have, I learned from him." What better tribute? An equally stirring tribute from Fields: "Bert Williams is the funniest man I ever saw and the saddest man I

Bert Williams

ever knew." Fields hit the crux of the matter with his deep insight. Williams was a displaced person. He wanted desperately to be accepted by everyone, yet he was discriminated against by whites. He was a West Indian who didn't quite feel at home with the American blacks, which was the reason his partner George Walker always felt so much more at ease playing black neighborhoods than did Williams.

Williams couldn't ignore the pain of the discrimination that had always plagued and puzzled him. How could "The King of Comedy" be so beloved by audiences while onstage and so discarded by them when offstage? One time when he was a <u>Follies</u> star, he was given permission to stay at a New York luxury hotel—if he would use the back elevator only. That New Year's Eve, he and Eddie Cantor went back to the hotel together. As the young Jewish comic, fresh out of a Jewish ghetto, and his buddy, who was forced to remain in one, reached the hotel, Williams headed for the back door. As they looked at each other, gulping back the pain, Williams said: "It wouldn't be so bad, Eddie, if I didn't still hear the applause in my ears."

On another occasion, the two chums from the <u>Follies</u> went into a bar in Louisville, where the show was playing on the road. As the bartender approached, he warned Cantor that Williams's drink would cost fifty dollars, hoping that would send the black man running, since he obviously didn't want to serve him. Williams grinned and reached into his pocket. Taking out a five-hundred dollar bill, he placed it on the bar and said, "Give me ten."

A tormented man who was the toast of Broadway when onstage and a "nigger" when offstage, Williams found it harder and harder to reconcile the two existences. He took to drinking heavily and went into deep depressions, unable to explain to himself why his audiences screamed for more but wouldn't allow him to enter or leave by the front door.

He worked himself harder and longer, as if that would somehow make the world accept him. It was as if he were trying to buy their acceptance with performances; the

BERT WILLIAMS

more he gave, the better were his performances—possibly they would finally accept him. In the end, Williams literally worked himself to death. He was seriously ill in 1918 when he performed in Ziegfeld's Midnight Follies and also at the Palace Theatre, working a double load. It wasn't long before he was forced to take a leave of absence and rest up in a sanitarium. No sooner was he back on his feet than he again took on the Follies of 1919 and a midnight show. He ended up back in the sanitarium. Somewhat rested, he again returned to Broadway and financed his own revue, Broadway Brevities.

Williams grew weaker by the day. By 1921 he was ready to drop, but he wouldn't give in. He wanted the public's acceptance, and this was the only way he knew how to get it. Although he had pneumonia, he still insisted on rehearsing for his latest starring role in a new comedy in which he was the only black, Under the Bamboo Tree. On February 25, 1922, he got through the matinee by sheer courage and made it halfway through the evening performance before collapsing. Within a week he was dead. As his body lay in state, mourners could see the symbol of his acceptance by a white people who embraced him as a person: his Masonic medallion. It had been twenty years since his brief visit to a land where he was nearly an equal.

The burning desire within Bert Williams to be loved and accepted by all finally put out his fire. He prophetically wrote his own epitaph in the lyrics of his greatest hit, "Nobody":

When life seems full of clouds and rain,
And I am full of nothin' but pain,
Who soothes my thumpin', bumpin' brain?
Nobody!

Bert Williams was forty-seven when he passed away.

MILLER & LYLES

MILLER & LYLES

Another all-black comedy team to attain stardom in the theater was Flournoy Miller and Aubrey Lyles. The first black act to do comedy without either singing or dancing, they merely walked out onstage and did their routine.

Flournoy and Aubrey met in Nashville in 1909 while both were attending Fisk University. Aubrey Lyles was a journalism major, and Flournoy was into music and writing. Through their mutual talents, they began writing and performing for school shows. Their first school shows were comedies based on political events. Quite often this became a spoof on the process of government. This type of satire was to remain part of their repertoire for the rest of their lives. The natural rapport and mutual admiration they held for each other made them a good comedy team. Flournoy was the tall handsome one with quite fair skin and a mellow deep voice; Aubrey was a complete contrast, being a short and dark-complexioned black man with a funny, squeaky voice that rattled when he became excited.

The difference between the two famous comedy acts, Williams and Walker and Miller and Lyles, was that Williams was the slow-witted one with the shuffling walk and he was always the one to get into trouble. Walker, the dark one, was usually the conniving dandy. Miller, on the other hand, was the city slicker who was always duping the little guy, Lyles. Lyles, the underdog, always went along with Miller on his schemes, but when the plans didn't work out, he was able to rattle his strange voice in such a way that it would break up the house with laughter. It was this combination that worked so well. They were both good writers and they knew their subject matter. Instead of using the minstrelsy type of talk, they did what is known as "Mutilatin' the Language." Phrases such as "I'm disgusted with you," became "I's reee-gusted wid chu."

During their college days, Miller and Lyles were the hit of the campus. However, the time between sessions provided them with an opportunity to take their talents to the houses. They would visit the Pekin Theatre in Chicago

Aubrey Lyles and Flournoy Miller

Miller and Lee

because they knew it had good shows and was known for the kind of entertainment provided by top-name black stars.

During the summer of 1911, when Ernest Hogan was appearing at the Pekin Theatre, they approached him with a sketch they wrote called "The Oyster Man." Hogan was very impressed by it and he showed it to the theater manager, Bob Motts. After reading the material, Motts also became excited and decided to try these two young men and their new fresh writing. Ernest Hogan starred in a production of "The Oyster Man," and the sketch was a huge success.

Afterward, Motts encouraged Miller and Lyles to write another project, which he would produce. This time they came up with a political satire called "The Mayor of Dixie." Ernest Hogan read and liked it very much. However, a previous commitment kept him from playing the role, so he suggested to Bob Motts that Miller and Lyles might take the starring roles in the show themselves. It was agreed, and the team of Miller and Lyles had its first chance.

"The Mayor of Dixie" was about two grocery clerks who wanted to run for mayor of Jimtown. This was the first showing of the talent of these two men who were to become very famous. The top reviewers in Chicago at that time were Amiel Leslie and Ashton Stevens. Both gave the show and the two new comedians plaudits. The show attracted the best people in town, including a society matron, Mrs. Potter Palmer. One night she reserved the entire theater for one of her charity functions. Miller and Lyles were such a hit with Chicago's society people that they were nearly adopted and, under the wing of Mrs. Palmer, they were on the road to stardom.

After the hit at the Pekin Theatre, the team opened their first vaudeville show at the Majestic Theatre in downtown Chicago. This was the Midwest's top vaudeville house. Later they went on to play in both the famous circuits, the Orpheum and the Keith. When they finally landed at Oscar

MILLER & LYLES

Hammerstein's in New York City, they were seen by George Lederer, the famed impresario, who immediately signed them up to appear in his new production, <u>Charity Girls</u>. It was while working in this show that they began thinking about doing their own shows again.

With much encouragement from their fans, they decided to resurrect their first hit, "The Mayor of Dixie," and take it to Broadway. Plans were made to enhance the show from what it originally was. They wanted additional music and dancing girls, but they had to be the most beautiful girls in the country—beautiful brown-skinned girls. In their search for a musician who could write additional tunes, they decided to look up an old friend, Jim Europe, a society band leader with the only black society band in New York City. Jim Europe suggested that they use his piano player. They took his advice and hired him. The piano player turned out to be Eubie Blake, who later became quite famous. They also hired Noble Sissle, a song-and-dance man who was also a song-plugger, to play the lead character, Tom Sharper. The next change was the name of the show. Times had changed and it was no longer fashionable to give your show a down-home feeling, so the show now had the bright fresh title of <u>Shuffle Along</u>.

In the 1920s, theaters maintained a strong policy on segregation in all the American cities. Although Miller and Lyles played the white vaudeville circuits, they were the only black act on the bill. When <u>Shuffle Along</u> came along, there were no blacks on Broadway. It was very difficult to get backing for a black musical, because show business backers felt that whites didn't want to sit next to black people in the theater. It was all right for the white folks to come to Harlem and sit next to the black people, and it was common in the 1920s for many of the upper-class whites to go "slumming" in Harlem nightclubs to hear black musicians perform, but the reverse was unacceptable.

Most of the financing money for <u>Shuffle Along</u> came from Miller and Lyles themselves. They had an advantage

MILLER & LYLES

in that they were established stars and were able to get dates in order to finance their show. With interest in black musicals drying up, they looked up a booking agent friend, Al Meyer. They knew him well and, more important than that, they trusted him. Meyer not only contributed advice, but he put up enough money to get the show into production.

Broadway bookings, however, were nil. In order to keep the cast together, the team began a series of one-nighters in black areas in New Jersey and Pennsylvania. But it was still difficult to entice white audiences. Even though the show was tremendously received in the black areas, white producers were reluctant to book it into the white houses. Short of money, they were unable to hire advance men to precede the show to drum up business. Each show was like another opening night. The production received good reviews, but played to small audiences. Local people never heard of the show until after it left town. With all these problems, it returned to New York to open in a broken-down musical hall in Sixty-Third Street, a small step from Harlem, but still a long way from the Broadway theater district.

Once Shuffle Along opened in the Sixty-Third Street Theatre, the show no longer shuffled along, it took off. The plot of this show was really unimportant because the humor relied on the minstrel show's caricatured dialect, rollicking slapstick, and empty-headed convoluted misuse of words: the "dese," "dems," and "does" of the stereotypical black language.

Another aspect of the show that contributed greatly to its success was the songs, including: "I'm Just Wild About Harry," "Love Will Find a Way," "Shuffle Along," "Gypsy Blues," and "If You've Never Vamped a Brownskin Vamp, Then You've Never Vamped At All."

The most important happening that created great interest was the dancing. It was a virtual compilation of all the dances featured on the black vaudeville circuit, but new to most white audiences. The time steps, the buck and wing,

MILLER & LYLES

soft-shoe, rapid-fire tap dancing, flips, somersaults, and twisting shimmy dances were performed with vitality and left the audience breathless. Everybody in the show danced, from the chorus to the main acts. They danced with tremendous speed, interchanging shuffling with buck and wing and various acrobatic numbers. Each show left the cast completely exhausted by the finale.

It was in this show that Miller and Lyles created their famous blackboard routine, in which Miller tries to tell Lyles that seven goes into thirteen twenty-eight times, and then proves it. This same routine was done by "Pigmeat" Markham on "The Ed Sullivan Show" many years later.

The word spread quickly of the new show Shuffle Along. The box office was swamped with people trying to buy tickets for what was now a smash hit. Thousands of people crowded the sidewalk in front of the Sixty-Third Street Theatre, creating enormous traffic jams. It was so bad that the New York traffic commissioner had to make Sixty-Third Street a one-way street. The show ran for over two years and after its New York success, plans were made to take it on the road. But Miller and Lyles had other ideas: they decided to leave the show to resume their careers in vaudeville.

In 1923 Miller and Lyles wrote another show called Runnin' Wild. In this one they introduced the new dance craze the Charleston. It was here that they discovered that they had a dancing girl at the end of the chorus line who did her routine in a very wacky manner. Her color was darker than the other girls and her distinctive dance style developed into something very exciting. They decided to keep her on the end of the line. The girl's name was Josephine Baker, who later became the toast of the Parisian music halls.

Again, this started a new fad to have a funny girl at the end of the chorus line. In the minstrel shows, the endmen provided the comedy. Now the endgirls were used to provide comedy relief in the musical shows.

MILLER & LYLES

Although Miller and Lyles constantly presented a new concept in comedy, the comedy still remained in black-face. The laughs were still created by the blackface comedian.

A few years later, between shows, they were asked to do a radio show from Chicago for Log Cabin Syrup. They were selected because they were the favorite comedians of most Chicagoans. Radio was a new dimension for show business, and they were hiring most of their talent from the vaudeville stage. Radio station WGN wanted Miller and Lyles because of their popularity. Harry Bestry, then their manager, negotiated the entire contract.

It was at that moment when the executives of the syrup company and the radio network saw that Miller and Lyles were not white that, after much discussion, they admitted that there had been a mistake. No deal. Again, it was the burnt cork masks on their faces each night that hid the fact that they were black men. Blackface was acceptable, but black skin was not.

Miller and Lyles returned to vaudeville, and this time were signed for another show called Great Temptation, produced by the great Shubert. For this new show they began to look for a new twist to their act, something different from their regular routine. It was Miller who developed the now-famous "Indefinite Talk" routine. It was a bit he had created in one. (In the theater, "in one" means to work in front of the drop curtain and down front stage.) It was a spot in the show that needed a bit that could be done in less than fifteen minutes and wouldn't need any props or sets, just talk. "Indefinite Talk" is two people talking together in a normal conversation with neither one letting the other complete a sentence without the other picking up the conversation on the last word.

The comics enter from each side of the stage with their greeting for each other, then:

MILLER & LYLES

Indefinite Talk

MILLER: What's wrong wid it?

LYLES: I just had it worked on.

MILLER: Who worked on it?

LYLES: De man who got the garage around—

MILLER: Oh. He ain't no good. De man you want is de man—

LYLES: I had him. He de one dat ruined it.

MILLER: Well, I see you got plenty of water . . . but you're out of gas.

LYLES: Oh, it ain't dat, I think maybe—

MILLER: No, it couldn't be dat!

LYLES: Well, it ain't much wrong wid it.

MILLER: What you need is some of those new gadgets, de kind that you buy—

LYLES: I just bought some.

MILLER: Oh, not them. I mean the kind that fastens where they fits, a whole dozen will cost you 'bout—

LYLES: That's too much money. I can't afford it. I got to get something that cost no more—

MILLER: You can't get it that cheap!

LYLES: We can get the car fixed up for maybe a-round—

MILLER: No. What you need is . . . a new car.

LYLES: Yeh!

MILLER: Kinda like the kind my uncle had when he went on a trip out dere—

LYLES: Did he go out dere?

MILLER: Sho!

LYLES: I thought all de time he was going to go—

MILLER: He did, but not that time.

LYLES: What's he doin' now?

MILLER: Well, since he's been back, he's been very busy gettin' ready for what he thinks is—

MILLER & LYLES

LYLES: Is dat so?

MILLER: Sho.

LYLES: Well, I guess like all bachelors, he's—

MILLER: No, not him! He's gonna get married—

LYLES: He is?

MILLER: Yeh, he gonna marry de widow whose husband use to—

LYLES: She's a fine lady. Listen, I heard that she—

MILLER: That was her daughter.

LYLES: Oh.

MILLER: You see, I'm keeping company wid her—

LYLES: You is?

MILLER: Yeh. I've been engaged to her now ever since the time—

LYLES: Yeh? I didn't know you knowed her dat long.

MILLER: Sho.

LYLES: I work with her brother and one day on the job the first thing I know—

MILLER: That's your fault . . . now what you should have done was—

LYLES: I did!

MILLER: You see, that's why I like to talk to you.

LYLES: Yeh?

MILLER: 'Cause you and me seems to agree wid one another . . . sho—

LYLES: You know one thing—when I gets the car fixed up, I'm to take you and your gal out for a ride sometime—

MILLER: That'll be great. Can you make it on next—

LYLES: I'll be busy then.

MILLER: Well, can you make it—

LYLES: Well, let's see . . . the best day for me—

MILLER: That suits me. What hour?

LYLES: Anytime between—

MILLER: That's a little early, but we'll be there.

LYLES: All right, I'll be seeing you.

MILLER: So long.

MILLER & LYLES

The comedy team of Amos 'n' Andy was the great sensation of radio starting in the late 1920s. When CBS and Log Cabin Syrup rejected Miller and Lyles because of their black skin, they did not throw out the idea of the show. They began to look for two white performers who could imitate black folks and create an act similar to Miller and Lyles's.

Two white vaudeville performers living in Chicago, Charles Correll and Freeman Gosden, auditioned for the parts and were chosen. The show was originally called "Sam and Henry." The amusing part of this was that Correll and Gosden were great fans of Miller and Lyles. They had been watching them perform for many years. The audition for them was a snap. All they did was recite the lines from one of Miller and Lyles's acts.

A few years later, Correll and Gosden decided to leave WGN because of a better offer from the Pepsodent Company and they moved to station WLS, on what was then called the Blue Network. They found that they could not retain the name "Sam and Henry" because the rights to that name were owned by WGN. Therefore, they had to come up with another name for their act. It was here that the famous names of Amos 'n' Andy began.

WGN tried to continue the show without Correll and Gosden, but they could not find the proper performers. The show was soon canceled.

While "Amos 'n' Andy" was creating a huge success, Miller and Lyles continued to work in vaudeville. Their success continued and it wasn't long before another radio station and a sponsor wanted to talk to them about a radio show similar to "Amos 'n' Andy." Miller made all of the contacts and because of his light skin, the question of race rarely came up. But when the final meeting and the signing of the contracts was held, Lyles was in the room and the sponsors backed out. This sealed their fate in that they would never appear on radio as a comedy team.

MILLER & LYLES

Mark Hellinger wrote in the <u>Chicago Daily Mirror</u> in October 1930 what probably described the case of Miller and Lyles as well as anyone could.

A newspaper on my desk goes into ecstacy over "Amos 'n' Andy," and lists a few of the team's contributions to American slang: "I's regusted, Ain't dat sumpin, sho, Ah is blue, unlax, it all depends on da sitcha-ation yo is in, ah ain't gonna do it.

Far be it from me to harbor any doubts about an American institution such as "Amos 'n' Andy." But it seems to me that they're two boys who are cashing in heavily on something Miller and Lyles originated many years ago. It is also surprising to me that Miller and Lyles haven't registered a squawk long before now. Miller and Lyles are two colored boys who have been Broadway stars for years. One is tall and has a deep voice and the other is short and delivers lines in a nervous sort of squeak.

For more years than I care to remember, I can recall Miller and Lyles using lines like "I is regusted." "It all depends on da sitcha-ation you is in," and similar construction, so similar in fact that the resemblence is uncanny. If Miller and Lyles were substituted for Amos and Andy one night, I would defy anyone could tell the difference. All the credit in the world to Amos and Andy. Ever since last August they have had this nation in hysterics. When I tune in on them and see my neighbors going into fits of laughter, I often wonder what Miller and Lyles are thinking about the success of Amos and Andy.

With all the rejections in radio, Aubrey Lyles became disenchanted with the discrimination against the black man in America. He joined the Marcus Garvey Movement,

Eubie Blake and Flournoy Miller

Charles Correll and Freeman Gosden as "Amos" and "Andy"

a movement to get blacks to return to their African home-land. He left for Africa without even informing Miller and stayed there for over a year. Upon learning of Lyles's departure, Miller became desperately ill with what he called Lobo pneumonia. His heart was broken over the departure of his partner and everybody feared for his life.

Upon his recovery producer Lew Leslie asked Miller to write the entire act for a new edition of Blackbirds, which would star Ethel Waters. Miller sought out another partner and teamed up with Mantan Moreland to recreate his famous skit, "Indefinite Talk." This activity kept Miller busy until 1933 when Lyles returned from Africa.

The team was reunited and one of the first decisions they made was to do another version of Shuffle Along. As they went into rehearsals, Lyles became very sick with peritonitis. He died before the show ever opened. The shock of losing his partner at a time like this was very hard on Miller. The task of casting the entire show now fell on his shoulders. In true show business tradition (the show must always go on), he contacted Mantan Moreland again and Shuffle Along opened to another long successful run.

In 1939 Flournoy Miller decided to move to the West Coast. He thought that the time may have come when the black comedian could remove his blackface. When he arrived in California, he found that it was difficult to get work in films. He just looked too white. In those days it was difficult to be funny by using a black dialect when your skin was too light in color. Needing to work and in desperation, he took a plunge into films by becoming a writer-producer. His initial venture was a film called Harlem on the Prairie, which starred a young and handsome vocalist-actor named Herb Jeffries. It also featured the comedy of Flournoy Miller and Mantan Moreland. They played two cops, and they didn't wear blackface.

Miller's writing became more prolific and he soon became one of the busiest freelance writers in the motion picture industry. In 1943 he assisted in the preproduction writing and appeared in Stormy Weather. It was in this

MILLER & LYLES

show that he recreated his famous "Indefinite Talk" routine with Johnny Lee. This, of course, was done in blackface.

After this, ironically enough, he began to write for the "Amos 'n' Andy Show," a relationship that was to last for eighteen years. In 1948 "Amos 'n' Andy" came to television. In its original form, it was two white men in blackface, but this would not work. A black cast, including a black Amos and a black Andy, had to be found. Flournoy Miller, who at this time was the head writer, was asked to cast the show. Fate works in strange ways. He picked a fine black comedian, Tim Moore, to play the part of Kingfish. It was perfect casting and Tim Moore became a hit. The sound that most comics use today to obtain a certain black effect, is adopted from the old Kingfish sound. "Sapphire, if your Mama was the Lone Ranger, she'd be alone alonnnng time!"

Flournoy was a great stalwart of show business. He loved it, lived it, and gave it his best at all times. He created some of the funniest comedy sketches ever written or spoken. He always insisted that the black performer should be treated with respect and dignity. It was during the time he was appearing in vaudeville and was well respected by managers and theater owners that he was able to influence them through the efforts of the Keith circuit to add the rules and regulations that the theaters passed out to the cast of the show. It read, "No one should use derogatory terms on the stage, such as <u>coon</u>, <u>darky</u>, or <u>nigger</u>, or any name that would be considered derogatory to the Negro race." To do so would mean instant cancellation, and it was strictly enforced.

Flournoy Miller was a giant of a man who loved mankind. He was black and proud of it. It was through his talents and efforts, always with a touch of humility, that he earned respect from all, not only for himself, but for all black entertainers. Flournoy Miller died in June 1971 at the age of eighty-one.

TOBA CIRCUIT

TOBA CIRCUIT

After World War I, many changes took place that were to affect the lives of black comedians and their humor for many years to come. Bert Williams, the epitome of the top black comedian, had left the black show circuits to work with such white extravaganzas as the Ziegfeld Follies.

The 1920s presented a new and different challenge to the black entertainer. The country was in an uplifting mood but the segregation doors were still closed and, consequently, the humor of the black man was changing during this period. New words and phrases were being developed that would soon become part of our everyday language.

Adding these new comedy routines to the new dances and songs, the black performer was able to put together new shows that toured the black sections of the major cities of the United States. This circuit tour, put together by the theater owners and the booking agents, was called the TOBA, which stood for Theatre Owners' Booking Association. As time passed, this also became known as the Toby Circuit or Toby Time. Sometimes the TOBA stood for "Tough on Black Asses," too.

This new theater circuit took the black performers throughout midwestern and southern cities. It hit the major black theaters in Chicago, Baltimore, Atlanta, Dallas, and many other cities in between. This circuit provided the black comedian with a place to perform and develop his routines and style. New words and phrases created on the Toby not only were to become part of the white entertainer's language, but part of America's street language.

The shows on this circuit were a combination of singers, dancers, and comedians. The comedian was the most important part of the show, so the show with the best comic was usually the most successful. They were always booked into theaters located in the black area of town, which also meant that their audiences were always black. In spite of this, the black comic had become so well identified with the image of the blackface comedian that he still put on the blackface.

TOBA CIRCUIT

Working the Toby Circuit was very hard. Performers had to put on two shows a day, and they usually had to do a lot of the other setup work in the theater. The performers traveled from city to city on trains that were segregated by sections at the time. Some of the more successful road shows were able to charter their own trains, which gave them an opportunity to live on board even while they were in a city for a week or more of performances.

These performers were booked to do their own two shows a day seven days a week, and quite often fifty-two weeks per year. This provided them with income and work for a year, but the pace was grueling. Some of the black performers were able to cross over into the white vaudeville circuit if they had the talent. There they did their same blackface routines that had become standard throughout the country. The big difference between their acts before a white audience and a black one was in the tone and quality of the segregation jokes.

Most of the comic routines consisted of two blackface comedians talking to each other, not to the audience. One would be the straight man and the other the comic. Although the comics always provided the entertainment between the musical numbers, they were usually the most popular part of the show. Quite often the comics would add other people (girls, usually) and develop their routines into short skits. A number of these skits became famous and were even adopted by white comedians for their shows. One of the most famous was the "Here Come de Judge" skit that Sammy Davis, Jr., later made famous on television. This was originally done by Pigmeat Markham on the Toby Circuit.

Additionally, a type of show called the tabloid was created on the Toby Circuit. It was different from the stock show in that it had a musical theme throughout, and in the finale the entire company participated in a production number that was based on the comedy of the show.

Ethel Waters was known as Sweet Mama Stringbean on the Toby Circuit and performed with a duo known as

"Midnight and Daybreak"

"Butterbeans and Susie"

Pigmeat and Freddie

Dusty Fletcher, George Wiltshire, and Sandy Burns

TOBA CIRCUIT

Butterbeans and Susie. They were one of the first man and woman teams.

Among the many black performers on this circuit were such famous names as Moss and Frye, who originated a unique comedy routine called Dumb Talk, which went like this:

How high is up?
Up where?
Up anywhere.

If you want to go to the railroad station
to buy a ticket, where are you going?
Hush, you don't know.
How many turns in a wheel?
Shut up, you're dumb!

Now let me ask you something. Say all you know. It'll only take a minute.
All right, if you had five dollars and I'd give you twenty more, what would you have?
I'd have a fit!

Willie Bryant and Leonard Reed called their act Brains and Feet because they introduced a great amount of dancing. Two others who left their mark were Ed Lee and Lincoln Perry. They starred in a show called "Step and Fetch It." Perry later adopted the name Stepin Fetchit and became quite a star playing the role of the lazy but clever nigger in motion pictures.

In 1925 the comedy team of Rastus Murry and Henry Drake developed a comedy routine that they used on the Toby Circuit called "Go Ahead And Sing."

Go Ahead and Sing

These two men are broke and they're trying to get themselves some money. One of them devises a plan on

TOBA CIRCUIT

how to get it. He tells the other that since one of them has talent, all he has to do is start singing. It would attract a crowd and, while he is singing, the other will pass the hat around and collect the money.

They agree, so one of the men starts to bark on the street: "Hey, everybody, gather around. You're gonna hear the greatest singer in the world!" Then in an aside to his partner, he says, "Now you sing, and you sing good."

The singer of the two starts into his song, and, after the first few bars of "My Wild Irish Rose," he's stopped by his friend.

"Hey, wait a minute," says the friend, "you can't sing no Irish song, you're in Harlem. Sing something that is down to earth, something that the folks up here will dig. You dig?"

He then starts into a blues song and is into the first few bars of it when the policeman comes up and stops him.

COP: Hey, you can't sing around here!

FIRST MAN: Who you're talkin' to, me?

COP: Yes, you, or him. You can't sing around here.

FIRST MAN: You talk to him. I'm not doin' nothin', I'm just standin' here.

COP: I wanna explain something to you. There's a hospital down the street. It has a lot of sick people in there and you're disturbing them. If you want to sing, go to another corner, but you can't sing here.

SINGER: Yes, sir, I won't sing here.

COP: You understand, then?

SINGER: Oh, yes, sir—yes, sir.

After the cop leaves the singer turns to his friend.

SINGER: All right. Let's go.

FIRST MAN: Go where? Why should we go anywhere? We're citizens. We've got a right to stand

here and sing, too. Ain't no flatfoot gonna tell us what to do. You go ahead and sing. When he comes back, I'll talk to him.

SINGER: You sure it's all right?

FIRST MAN: Sure, it's all right. You go ahead, sing!

He then starts to go into his song. As he starts to sing, the cop comes back.

COP: Wait a minute. Didn't I just tell you not to sing on this corner?

SINGER: Yes, I know, Officer, but my partner said it was all right.

COP: I don't care what your partner said. I said you can't sing here. This is the last time I'm gonna tell you. If I have to come back again, I'm gonna take this billy and put it upside your head. Then I'm gonna take you to jail!

The cop turns to walk away.

FIRST MAN: You ain't gonna hit me in my head.

COP: What?

He starts to beat the singer over the head with the billy stick.

COP: Now let that be a lesson to you!

SINGER: (holding his head) Yes, cap'n, yes, sir!

FIRST MAN: (as the cop starts to leave) You got a lot of nerve, hitting a citizen. You ain't gonna hit me no more.

The cop comes back and hits the singer on his feet, and the other one starts to agitate. The singer then proceeds to beat the other man off the stage. Blackout.

There were many other classic routines developed during this time that became standards in comedy for years,

TOBA CIRCUIT

like the one-dollar-pays-all-the-debts routine of Jules McGarr.

Two Dollars Bit

This bit is done with a comic, a straight man, and a woman. The straight man meets the comic on the street:

STRAIGHT MAN: Look, I've been waiting for you a long time. I let you have two dollars a long time ago, and you never returned my money. I need my money and I need it bad. Now give me my two dollars.

COMIC: Well, to be truthful, I've only got one dollar. Tell you what I'm gonna do. I'm gonna give you this one dollar and the next time I see you, I will give you the other one. How zat?

STRAIGHT MAN: Well, okay, but I want my money the next time I see you.

The comic exits. As the straight man gets ready to exit at the opposite side, he meets a girl.

GIRL: I sure have been waiting for you a long time. Do you remember when you asked me to loan you two dollars and I did? But you've never returned my money. Now I see you got some money.

STRAIGHT MAN: Well—I only got this dollar, but I'm gonna give it to you, and the next time I see you I'll give you the other dollar.

GIRL: Well, okay, but remember, I want my money the next time we meet.

He gives her the dollar and exits. As she starts to leave from the opposite

side, she meets the comic. He was coming back as he spots her.

COMIC: Oh, am I glad to see you! Remember that two dollars I loaned you and you never gave it back? I see you got some money now, and I need my money.

GIRL: Well, I only got this dollar.

COMIC: Well, I'll take it and the next time we meet, I'll get my other dollar.

He takes the dollar and she exits. As the comic starts to leave, he runs into the straight man coming back.

STRAIGHT MAN: Oh, I see you got my dollar. Hey, thanks.

As the comic leaves, the straight man runs into the girl.

GIRL: Oh, I see you got my other dollar.

The straight man exits, and the girl runs into the comic.

COMIC: Oh, I see you got my other dollar. Now, that makes us all straight!

The comic is paid off and now he's got the one dollar that he started out with; everybody's paid up. Blackout.

The Checkers Bit (By Gulf Port and Brown)

This was a very short bit, done always after the opening of the show. The stage is completely dark and all you hear is the sound of footsteps. The two men are walking and the first speaks up:

TOBA CIRCUIT

VOICE ONE: Halt, who goes there?
VOICE TWO: Nobody.
VOICE ONE: Go ahead.

> Footsteps are heard as they walk up-stage. They sit down.

VOICE ONE: Uh-huh, I gotcha.
VOICE TWO: You got who, you dirty rat.
VOICE ONE: I got you, you dirty dog.
VOICE TWO: I've waiting a long time to get you in this spot. Now I've got you.
VOICE ONE: I've got you cornered, and you're never gonna get out of here.
VOICE TWO: Oh yeh, well, make a move and I'll kill you.
VOICE ONE: Who me?
VOICE TWO: Make a move. Damn you, move!
VOICE ONE: Who me?
VOICE TWO: Yes, you.
VOICE ONE: Who me?
VOICE TWO: Move. Move!

> The lights go up and reveal two men playing checkers. One jumps over the other's man. Blackout.

Western Union Bit

CLERK: No, no, I want to know the address so I can send your telegram.
EDDIE: Oh, okay. 424 Sherman Row—in the rear.
CLERK: What city?
EDDIE: Bessemer, Alabama.
CLERK: Okay, what's the message?
EDDIE: "I arrived in New York City and I have found everything all right. I will send you some money tomorrow. I am living on Long Island.

Your loving brother. Hallowed."

CLERK: What was the name?

EDDIE: Hallowed.

CLERK: Strange name.

EDDIE: It's from the Bible.

CLERK: From the Bible?

EDDIE: You never read the Bible, "Our Father, who art in heaven, Hallowed be thy name"? How much do I owe you?

CLERK: (while he counts the words, he does a sing-song undertone) That will be twenty-four dollars and ten cents.

EDDIE: Twenty-four dollars and ten cents?

CLERK: I could show you how to save some money. You see, you've got a lot of useless words here that you don't really need.

EDDIE: How much can you save me?

CLERK: Oh, I don't know. Let me see. More than half.

EDDIE: Okay, save me.

CLERK: Well, this first sentence. You say, "I arrived in New York City." You don't have to say all that. Just say you've arrived. Then—"and I have found everything all right." Now all you got to say is "Found everything okay." Then you say, "I will send you some money tomorrow." Instead, say, "Money coming. Living on L.I."

EDDIE: What's that L.I.?

CLERK: That's my way of saying Long Island.

EDDIE: My sister ain't gonna know nothing about you. She'll be looking all over Alabama trying to find L.I. Say, "Living on Long Island."

CLERK: Now you've got, "Your loving brother." You don't need to say all that. Just say, "Loving brother."

EDDIE: All right, now read it.

CLERK: "Arrived safe. Found everything okay. Money coming. Living on Long Island. Loving brother, Hallowed."

TOBA CIRCUIT

EDDIE: That's fine. Now, how much do I owe you?

CLERK: (repeats the sing-song while adding up the words) Nine dollars and seventy-five cents.

EDDIE: What? You mean the more words you take out, it'll be less to send it?

CLERK: Yes, sir.

EDDIE: Well, see if we can take out some more words. Now, that first sentence, "Arrived safe." Well, I couldn't send a telegram if I wasn't here, could I? So leave that out. Now what you got?

CLERK: "Found everything okay."

EDDIE: She's gonna think I found everything and she's gonna want half of it and I ain't found nothing, so just cut that out. Now, what you got?

CLERK: "Money coming."

EDDIE: Now that's a lie. You know I don't have enough money to pay my rent, so you know I'm not going to send her nothing. Ain't no use lying to my sister, so take that out. Now, what you got?

CLERK: "Living on Long Island."

EDDIE: Now that's gonna worry her to death. Like I said, she don't know nothing about Long Island. And she'll be wondering and I wouldn't want to do nothing to hurt my sister. So cut that out. Now what you got?

CLERK: "Loving brother, Hallowed."

EDDIE: I love my sister and my sister loves me. My sister is two years younger than me. Ever since we were born she's been like a sister to me. And we know we love each other. I love her and there ain't no use to keep on repeating it. Take it out. Now, what you got?

CLERK: Ain't nothing here now but your name, "Hallowed."

EDDIE: Send that. (turns to exit) Collect!

Blackout.

TOBA CIRCUIT

Ain't Nobody Here Either

Performed by Willie Too Sweet with the Whitman Sisters Show—1929.

Bedroom scene, with husband and wife. He's very jealous and warns her that he doesn't want anyone in the house while he's away. They're sitting on the bed as the scene opens.

HUSBAND: I'm leaving now, and I don't want nobody in this house while I'm gone. If the mailman comes with a letter, tell him to shove it under the door. If the milkman comes, tell him to take it back and bring it back later. If the iceman comes, tell him it's too hot, we don't need any.

WIFE: But we need ice. It's gonna be very hot.

HUSBAND: I don't care how hot it gets. Tell him to come back when I'm here, you understand?

WIFE: Yes, darling, but you know I never have a man in the house when you're away.

HUSBAND: I don't know. I've heard rumors.

WIFE: That's not true. No man has ever been here when you're not home.

HUSBAND: Well, make sure you keep it that way. I've got to get the fertilizer and put it on strong, and I don't want nobody here.

After he leaves, Jazzbo enters.

JAZZBO: Did he leave? I'm so glad he's gone.

As they start to hug, a knock on the door is heard.

WIFE: It's my husband coming back! He's so jealous. If he finds you here, I don't know what will happen.

JAZZBO: Oh my God, let me get outa here.

TOBA CIRCUIT

Jazzbo runs into the closet as the husband enters and starts to accuse his wife.

HUSBAND: There's a man in here, I know it.

WIFE: No, darling, there's no one here, I swear.

Husband starts to look behind the dresser, under the bed, under the table, and each time saying the same thing as he looks.

HUSBAND: You're right, ain't nobody here.

When he opens a closet door, there's a man standing there with two guns, one in each hand, pointing directly at him.

HUSBAND: You're right, ain't nobody here either!

Slams door shut. Blackout.

Eddie Green

Scene opens with a clerk at the desk in a Western Union office and Eddie walks in.

EDDIE: Good afternoon.

CLERK: Good afternoon, could I help you?

EDDIE: Yes, I'd like to send a telegram.

CLERK: All right, who do you want to send it to?

EDDIE: That's asking a lot, asking where I'm sending a telegram to. That's meddling, ain't it?

CLERK: Well, I can't very well send a telegram for you if I don't know where you want it sent to.

EDDIE: Well, in that case, I'm sending it to my sister.

CLERK: What's your sister's name?

EDDIE: That's none of your business. You just send it to my sister.

CLERK: Look, I can't send it until I know your sister's name.

EDDIE: Oh, okay, her name is Esmeralda.

Stephen Ciavelli

CLERK: How do you spell it?

EDDIE: You work here? You get paid for this?

CLERK: Yes.

EDDIE: Esmeralda.

Clerk begins to write it, then he asks—

CLERK: What's her address?

EDDIE: Now I know you're going too far now. Now you want to know her address. Now I guess you want to go down there and talk to my sister, huh?

CLERK: No, that's got nothing to do with it. I've got to know where to send the telegram, if I'm going to send it.

EDDIE: What you mean? You ain't got nothing to do with my sister? Who do you think you are? Nothing to do with my sister! Everybody got something to do with my sister.

Blackout.

The depression era saw the end of the Toby Circuit. Black theaters were quick to run into financial problems and close their doors. This led to an exodus of some of the top black stars to that part of the world known as Harlem and a particular theater there called the Apollo.

However, before the Toby Circuit disappeared completely, there were many more black stars who achieved fame. One of the most renowned was the great Bill Robinson. Although he was basically a dancer, it was on the Toby Circuit that he learned how to stand and amuse audiences with funny stories. He started this after hours with a group of actors, regaling them with one story after another. Soon after this, he began coming out on the stage after the finale and keeping the audiences in their seats for another twenty or thirty minutes by telling them a series of his latest stories. The people loved it. Many of his stories

Pigmeat and Freddie

John Mason on Stage at the Apollo Theatre

became classics and have been told hundreds of times. One of them was the one about the soldier:

> A soldier was trying to get off the base to visit his girlfriend in town. But at that time, no one was allowed off the base. As the soldier approached the sentry, he was halted by a "Who goes there?" The soldier replied, "Me." The sentry said, "No one's allowed off the base tonight," to which the soldier calmly replied, "Listen here, I got a mother in heaven, a father in hell, and a gal in Harlem, and damned if I ain't gonna see one of them tonight!

Another of Bill Robinson's famous stories was about another soldier who was told by his lieutenant to prepare for a hike.

> The lieutenant said, "Hey, Simpson, I want you to pack up all this gear, pick up your rifle, get all those knapsacks and canteens to carry on this fifty-mile hike." The soldier answered in a quivering voice, "Lieutenant, sir, did you call me? Do you know my name?" The lieutenant answered, "Simpson, I said Simpson." To which the soldier responded, "Oh, I thought you said Sampson."

Another comedy team that grew up on the Toby Circuit and was able to cross over into the white vaudeville shows was known as Glenn and Jenkins, and their routine identified another typical role that the black played in society. The setting involves two railroad porters in the station. Both are in blackface as they are seen sweeping the floor and talking to each other:

> "I got me a sweet letter from my girl, and she says she loves me."

Mantam Morland

While they are talking, the audience begins to concentrate on the broom, which is part of their act. It is manipulated in such a manner that part of the laughs are coming in response to the brooms and part by the verbal routine.

"I don't believe you."
"Well, read it for yo'self."

It becomes obvious that the partner cannot read, and tries to cover that fact.

"I can't read no rottin' writin'—read yo own writin' if it's rotten."
"Well, she writes to me that I is her flying black ace."
"She can talk plainer than dat."

Sammy Davis, Jr.

By this point the brooms are almost dominating the activity and the audience would be enjoying it all.

Several other famous blackface comedians who graduated from the Toby Circuit were Buck and Bubbles, Dusty Fletcher, Mantam Moreland, Time Moore, and the great Dewey "Pigmeat" Markham.

TOBA CIRCUIT

The Toby Circuit produced still another famous comic and singer, who started out in his uncle's act called "Hearts in Dixieland" in blackface at the age of four. The child-labor laws frowned on children being exploited on the stage, because it usually kept them from attending school. To avoid any possible trouble from the authorities, his uncle blackened his nephew's face and passed him off as a forty-four-year-old midget. His name was Sammy Davis, Jr. The following is a transcript of an interview with him.

"Comedy at that time was done by the great dialecticians of that era. The black style of comedy was the same for the black man as for the white man. You had the Jewish comics who wore baggy pants, the Dutch comedians who 'had accents that were so strong you could cut them with a knife, and then there was the Irish comic. All of the comedy in those days was ethnic because the country was full of immigrants, and the people always enjoyed the low-style comedy of their heritage. It was the same with the blackface comedian; he not only made people laugh at him and his people, he also made fun of other races and nationalities.

"This was the time when comedians never spoke directly to the audiences. They would always talk to their partners. There was never any direct eye contact with the audience, and they would never just walk out onto the stage and begin their routine. The usual format was something like this:

"After a production number, the band would strike up a bluesy-style tune. The curtains would close, and the comedians would walk onstage talking to each other. By the time the music had stopped, they had reached the center of the stage, with the audience slowly picking up their conversation. It gave the audience the feeling that they were participating in a private conversation between two people.

'I've never been so embarrassed in all mah life.'
'What did I do?'

TOBA CIRCUIT

'What did you do? When we was at the dinner table and that nice lady asked you to pass the black bass, you shoved me over to her.'

'And another thing. That time you told me that those two girls we dated were school teachers. How did you know they were school teachers?'

'Oh, I knew they were school teachers 'cause one didn't have no class and the other didn't have no principals.'

These were our style jokes at that time. It's like the old saying, 'Dem's de jokes, folks.'

"My concept of black humor is very nonracial, in a way, until it reaches the punch line. At that time I color it with typical black sounds. For instance, I pretend that I'm walking up to a desk clerk and, in a very white-style voice, I'll say, 'Good evening, my good man. My name is Sammy Davis, Jr. Do you have my reservation?' The desk clerk would answer, 'I don't have your reservation and I don't know you.' My answer, which would be the punch line, would be a switch to a typical black voice, 'Whatcha mean ya don't know me!' It's not the words that are funny, it's when I switch voices and become colored that is funny.

"I learned this by being with all kinds of people and relating to them. The fact that I am black and Jewish always gets a funny reaction from the audience. Like when I would say, 'I've been Jewish for twenty-two years and I've been black for, oh, about . . .' I don't even have to finish the line to get a laugh. It's the rhythm of the lines that is most important and everyone has their own rhythm. Most of the time it really does not have anything to do with the subject matter.

"I never considered blackface to be a put-down or degrading. I thought our theater, and especially the Toby Circuit, could stand up to anybody. It was the greatest training ground in the world for a performer, because when you left the Toby, you could play anywhere and anytime and be a success.

TOBA CIRCUIT

"I learned how to dance by watching great stars like Bill Robinson, Buck and Bubbles, and others. You naturally picked up comedy stories as you listened to them go through their routines. I began to imitate all the comedians that I saw. I would try to follow their words and also develop the sound of their voices. It was here that I began to do my first impressions. By the time my uncle, my father, and I became an act, I was doing takeoffs on all the stars.

"Jerry Lewis became my favorite impression and the audience would request him more than anyone else. I would also do Frank Sinatra and Dean Martin. By this time the act was called the 'Will Mastin Trio,' featuring Sammy Davis, Jr., and my impressions had become well known. When I finally branched off on my own, I added more talk and jokes to the act. Nipsey Russell would write some of my comedy lines; as I added that to my act, it all became part of my presentation.

"There were two things that I did in my acts that had a great impact on two of the old timers from the Toby Circuit. When I did the old 'Here Come de Judge' bit on the 'Laugh-In' show, it brought Pigmeat Markham to the attention of the public once again. It was one of those funny things that you say as we were sitting around with the 'Laugh-In' crew. We were trying to come up with something new when I said, 'Here come de judge.'' It was the rhythmic pattern that turned out to be funny. I told them that it wasn't my line, it was Pigmeat's. As a result of this, the producers had to pay Pigmeat $500 every time we used that bit. It also got Pigmeat dates at the Sands Hotel in Las Vegas and Harrah's Club in Lake Tahoe.

"The other old timer from the Toby Circuit who received some belated credit for his earlier efforts was a man by the name of Sam Theard. Sam was better known as Spo-Dee-O-Dee. I would open my show at Caesar's Palace with a movie film of me at age four singing, 'I'll Be Glad When You're Dead You Rascal You.' That song was written by Sam Theard.

TOBA CIRCUIT

"I think that one of the most profound things that ever happened to me in my whole career was when Bob Hope said to me, 'Where did you learn to be funny and black? Your timing is amazing. How did you learn it?' To me that was a supreme compliment. He also said, 'You can go back and forth and be just as funny when you reach back and go black.'

"There was a time when I had not realized that I was able to use the two groups. I would be very correct in my use of the English language while talking to one person and then I could easily drop into the sound of the brother, the dude on the corner. That cat can relate to me. I think that is the reason for the great success of Richard Pryor. He is so basic. He can do a dude type that all the black people know so well. He is the dude that hangs out in the poolroom or the barbershop or just on the street corner.

"I heard most of my early comedy backstage at the Apollo Theatre in Harlem. We didn't call them jokes at that time, we called them lies. 'That nigger sure can lie,' was a a common phrase at that time. I would imagine it is still used today. These backstage stories become parts of various routines for everyone. The Apollo Theatre became the mecca for so many black performers after the Toby Circuit closed down during the Depression. Without this work of the circuit, they came to Harlem and continued to perform. It was here in Harlem when the black comics gathered that black humor began to blossom and grow and set the stage for what it was to become after World War II."

Buck and Bubbles

TOBA CIRCUIT

Another black comic to develop his talents on the Toby Circuit was Sam Theard, better known as Spo-Dee-O-Dee. He began his career in New Orleans, where he was one of the dancers who followed the funeral processions. The following is a transcript of an interview with this great entertainer.

"I was a second-liner, which meant that I didn't even know who was dead. It was the music and the crowds that attracted me. The second-liners were the people who walked behind the mourners. The idea was to create your own style of walking. I think it was here that we began to have a strut. You usually waited until the band left the body off at the ceremony. As soon as the body was deposited, the band would walk about a block, the bass drum would give a signal and they would start to play jazz while we would strut down the avenue.

"When I first started in regular show business, I had to wear blackface. I never wanted to wear it, but they wouldn't play you if you didn't black up. I started out as a singer and always wanted to write my own songs, but I had to wear blackface in order to put my songs over. I had a fairly good voice in those days, and I could dance; so I was able to work on the Toby Circuit.

"My performing days really started when I was a kid. I built a stage in my backyard and would cast my friends in the parts that I wanted them to play. I began appearing in talent contests at the Lyric Theatre, an all-black theater on the Toby Circuit in New Orleans. Toby was a rough school, but it was the greatest place for a performer. I learned how to do skits, comedy, dance, and be part of the production. The shows that I worked were called tabs, short for tabloids. These were scaled-down versions of the musicals that played the big-time Toby Circuits.

"On the Toby you had to do everything. The singers and the dancers might have to do a situation comedy. The comedians would do a monologue or sing or do a parody. We had no money to hire writers in those days; we had to

Spo-De-O-Dee

write all our own shows and skits. After working in the Toby, you became a well-seasoned performer. It was here that I began to write my own tunes and use these songs to extend my comedy. I could always put a song into a funny situation whenever I wanted to.

"I remember my first show as a comedian and singer. It was in Pensacola, Florida, and I was singing in the Jolson style like everyone else. I would carry my hat in my hand, all rolled up in my white gloves, and try to bring tears to the audience. The white gloves were just as important as the blackface for all performers.

"I traveled the Toby Circuit in the South for many years and even took on a carnival job once. But the big break came to me when I was finally working in the North in Chicago, where I recorded my first tune on the Brunswick label, 'I'll Be Glad When You're Dead You Rascal You.' The stage name that I was using at that time was Lovin' Sam From Bam. Louis Armstrong recorded my song and it became one of his first hits. It was after this that I was booked into the Club DeLisa, where I wrote a song with suggestive lyrics:

TOBA CIRCUIT

There is one thing in the world that no one can do without
You know damn well what I am talking about,
Spo-Dee-O-Dee

And the band would answer: Spo-Dee-O-Dee

Everybody's doing it now.
The chickens would lay no eggs or flop no wing
If that ole rooster didn't have that certain thing.
Spo-Dee-O-Dee
Everybody's doing it now.

Well, the name stuck to me. That's why I tell everybody that Spo-Dee-O-Dee was born in the Club DeLisa in Chicago in 1938.

"In 1939 I decided to do my comedy routines without the blackface. I was one of the first black comedians that discarded the blackface, mainly because I just disliked it. When you went out after the show without it on, no one would recognize you. After this I went to the Apollo Theatre, where I did my own show. I wrote the whole thing in rhyme. We had Count Basie's band, and Moms Mabley played the woman in the skit. She was a washerwoman and I was coming over to get some of her money.

      'Hey, woman! Where's the money?'
She would reach her hand out and I would say in a stern voice,
      'Bring it over here, woman.'
She would try to hide some of the money from me and say,
      'I need the money for food.'
   'You ate yesterday. You want to eat every day?'
I was a cruel bastard as I took the money.
   'Here, woman, get yourself some saltine cracker
      and save some of them for me.'

"Our humor was ethnic, sexual, cruel, and, quite often, slapstick. We did just about everything to get laughs, and we usually did."

THE SCREEN'S FIRST COON

SCREEN'S FIRST COON

With the coming of the talking movies, Al Jolson brought the blackface comedian and singer to the screen in that famous film The Jazz Singer. That first talkie also brought on a demand for the black entertainer in motion pictures. The role that Jolson had created was to be repeated many times and become the classic format for the black comic's role on the screen. In 1929 the first all-black musical, Hearts of Dixie, was filmed. It starred a fine actor, Clarence Muse, and spotlighted the talents of a fast-rising comedian, Stepin Fetchit. He was six feet tall, lanky, and very dark. His head was clean-shaven and his eyes always looked as if they were dilated. This gave him the appearance of the old stereotyped slave character who was forever trying to find ways to avoid work—the standard and expected role of the coon character.

Step's career began to soar after his appearance in Hearts of Dixie. He was signed to a long-term contract by 20th Century-Fox, and he took the nation by storm. Between 1929 and 1935, Step made twenty-six films, sometimes working in four at the same time. He was the first black artist to receive feature billing and scenes were written especially for him. His contribution to black humor in the movies was as important as Bert Williams's was to the stage. During those years in films, he costarred with many famous white actors and actresses, such as Shirley Temple and Will Rogers.

The character he created in each of his films was generally the same. He wore pants that were always too big for him and looked as if they were going to fall at any moment. He usually played the part of a backward handyman who did odd jobs for his master. Often referred to as "the damndest nigger in the world," his slow shuffle and almost unintelligible dumb stammer not only became well known and loved by audiences all over the world, it also determined the type of role all blacks in the film industry were to play.

SCREEN'S FIRST COON

By the end of each picture, he would win over the master in a clever way and climax his success with a high-stepping number that made him look like a one-man carnival. This was the Stepin Fetchit character in the 1930s, and it affected motion picture comedy for more than a decade.

Step often said that he was the first to portray black characters that were acceptable to a Jim Crow society. The black audiences, however, began to reject him. They were finding his "coon" characters offensive and not in keeping with the new concepts of black people.

Step's fight with the civil rights groups had a definite effect on his career. He claimed it was he who elevated the black man in motion pictures and opened the doors to blacks being portrayed without blackface. Nonetheless, his concepts were no longer accepted, and before long, the doors to the film companies were closed to him.

When this happened he returned to the stage, and his name brought top billing. But time had taken its toll on his type of comedy; it was no longer accepted. His act consisted of a girl dressed as a bellhop rolling Step onstage in a wheelchair. The band played a fast tune, but Step was wheeled very slowly. Step said that this act "made me the only man in show business who made a million doing nothing."

During his stage career and after, he continuously drank Guinness stout by the case. He carried a bottle in each of his coat pockets. Those who knew him well realized that the slur in his talk was not part of the act, but the result of the stout.

With all his problems, Stepin Fetchit was indeed the man who opened Hollywood's doors for black entertainers. He opened theaters for them and made them first-class citizens. Step was a star and he did create a style that later brought forth two more fine black comedians, Willie Best and Mantam Moreland. Their comedy is considered Uncle

SCREEN'S FIRST COON

Tom today, but it had its place in the annals of black humor.

Comedy was undergoing changes at that time. The Tom style was being rejected in the 1930s, but, in ironic contrast, the blackface comedian still continued in the variety theater. This type of show was finding a place in the movie houses, where variety shows were presented onstage between showings of the film. These live shows still had black comics who, for reasons they considered important, remained in blackface.

THE APOLLO THEATRE

APOLLO THEATRE

The bandleader swings his musicians into the house's bright and brassy theme, "I May Be Wrong, But I Think You're Wonderful," someone backstage yells, "All on!" and a chorus line of lovely young ladies comes dancing out onstage. After precision kicks and struts, the "flash act"— usually dancers—appears. By this time, the audience is really settling in to enjoy the show. They know what's coming—the comics.

Sure enough, the music swells and the chorus line and dancers take their bows and exit with a flourish. Just as they do, the curtains pull closed and the stage is bare. But not for long. Out come two men in blackface. They walk toward each other, meet at centerstage, talk to each other —never acknowledging the audience but carrying them along with their every word. Someone in the second row anticipates what is coming and giggles. Someone hoots at the giggler. Then the straight man delivers the final setup, the comedian punches his gag line, and the entire house breaks up.

It's showtime at the Apollo. Magictime, when the audience forgets their troubles, their problems, their burdens. They laugh with the comedians, groove with the musical groups, swoon with the vocalists—but mainly they laugh with the comics. The Apollo Theatre—a landmark, an institution, a piece of living history, and the birthplace of almost every black performer, whether star, superstar, or legend—is a legend in its own right.

Smack in the middle of what is now considered the business and entertainment district of New York City's Harlem sits the world-famous Apollo Theatre. On the north side of 125th Street between Seventh and Eighth Avenues, the backbone of black show business still offers the best show around. It may not be the fanciest or the most plush showplace, but every black performer of any stature looks forward to playing there.

And the patrons would usually rather pay good money to see a star perform "In Person at the Apollo" than travel

APOLLO THEATRE

downtown to more lush surroundings to see the same act. The reason? The Apollo has an atmosphere all its own—and the audience makes up the biggest part of it. There is an electricity between the performers and the people they are trying to entertain, a bond as tight as brotherhood when an act gets it all together, and there is a pride in the theater. The Apollo belongs not just to the people of Harlem, but to blacks everywhere.

Although the people may consider the Apollo <u>their</u> theater, it was owned by Frank Schiffman, a white impresario who presented shows there for nearly a half-century, until his death. Well into his seventies, the elder Schiffman finally handed the running of the theater over to his sons Bobby and Jack, although Jack moved to Florida, leaving the theater in brother Bobby's capable hands.

Unlike many other owners of businesses in Harlem that are white owned and run, the Schiffmans insisted that the only thing white about the Apollo would be the owners. The stagehands and all personnel are black. For many years, the Apollo was the only theater in the country that hired black stagehands; in fact, the Harlem local of the International Association of Theatrical Stage Employees wouldn't even let its members seek work outside the Apollo.

Started in the early thirties by Schiffman and his very silent partner, Leo Brecher, in its heyday the Apollo offered thirty shows a week that included known musicians, a regular chorus line, and a top comedian. Times have changed, policies have changed—there are fewer shows per week now—but the electrifying excitement never changes. The entertainers are booked into the theater for two- or three-week engagements but can be held over if the audiences warrant it. Although the two-balcony theater is comparatively small—holding only 1,700 seats—well over 2,200 people can be crammed in to fill even standing-room areas and the aisles when a spectacular show hits town.

Spo-de-Odee at the Apollo Theatre

Top: A Chorus Line; bottom: Typical Singers and Dancers at
the Apollo

APOLLO THEATRE

The entrance to the second balcony, lovingly called the Buzzards' Roost, is kept separate from that of the first balcony and the orchestra so that people who have paid very little to climb the many flights of stairs to sit where the air is thick and hot can't slip down to the more expensive seats. But the second-balcony customers have a personality all their own, and they can often make or break an act by their deafening boos and hoots or their equally earsplitting cheers and applause. Most acts play to the second balcony in hopes of acceptance.

Even though the shows ran seven days a week, Wednesday night was always a crowd-pleaser—that was, and still is, amateur night. Acts come from all over to try their luck on amateur night. If they're successful and win first place, their prize is a treasure for any aspiring amateur: a one-week booking at the Apollo. Second prize is fifteen dollars, and third prize is ten dollars. Naturally, everyone shoots for that week at the Apollo and hopes they don't come in second or third—especially if they're part of a large group who will have to split the small money four, six, or even eight ways.

Some of the stars of today and yesterday who got their start in show business directly from the Apollo amateur night are: Billy Eckstine, Billie Holliday, Bill Kenny and The Ink Spots, Gladys Knight and the Pips, Barbara McNair, Leslie Uggams, and Sarah Vaughn and many, many more—well over 100. It has been claimed that Ella Fitzgerald was an Apollo amateur-night winner who got her start toward stardom there—but nearly every other theater and club in the country has made the same claim.

One of the big delights of amateur night—besides being able to heckle and whistle and clap and stomp—is a stagehand named Porto Rico. He throws a chill into the spines of the would-be performers, because if they aren't any good or aren't doing well, he comes right out onstage and gets them. At one time, he used a long rod with a hook at the end and hauled the poor dudes off bodily. Later, to

APOLLO THEATRE

add extra fun to the festivities, Porto Rico started "shooting" those who were bombing out. As the story goes, one night Norman Miller, a stagehand in charge of sound who had been renamed Porto Rico for when he gave the losers the hook, had his sensitive eardrums so badly pierced by someone's offkey attempt at singing that he frantically grabbed a nearby cap pistol and came out shooting. The audience loved it, so Porto Rico kept it in. Instead of the hook, he started coming out onstage in different costumes —dressed in a hula skirt with bare belly flapping, or padded bra and skirt—dancing circles around the failing act that's about to be "executed" with a pistol loaded with blanks. As soon as the audience catches sight of Porto Rico, they start hooting and yelling, and they're really howling by the time he finally shoots off the gun at the loser. Obviously, you take your own chances when you go out onstage on amateur night.

But Porto Rico wasn't always right. Once he was offended by some sour notes a young singer hit, and he danced out and "shot" him. Five weeks in a row the dude sang the same song, and five times Porto Rico shot him down. His name was Roy Hamilton, who soon afterward signed a big record contract and hit the top fast with his recording of "I'll Never Walk Alone," which was the song he sang at the Apollo. He may have been slightly offkey, but he was very much on the charts—but he never won at the Apollo.

There have been several Porto Rico's since Norman Miller. As one would retire, another would take his place. The latest one is played by comic Junkie Jones.

All the top black bands have played the Apollo Theatre: Count Basie, Duke Ellington, Lionel Hampton, Fletcher Henderson, Earl Fatha Hines, Chick Webb, Fats Waller. Most of the biggest tried to play there at least twice a year, and some still do. Schiffman also booked in the best of the white and mixed bands, too: Charlie Barnet, the Dorsey brothers, Benny Goodman, Woody Herman, Harry James,

APOLLO THEATRE

Gene Krupa, Guy Lombardo, Glenn Miller, Louis Prima, Artie Shaw—and the beat goes on and on and on.

Along with the best bands in the land to set the theater really jumping, the best vocalists were also drawn there. The great Josephine Baker, Cab Calloway, Nat King Cole, Ella Fitzgerald, Johnny Mathis, Dinah Washington, Nancy Wilson, and so many more. The fabulous Lena Horne only played the Apollo once—back in 1934 for $35 for the week as vocalist for Noble Sissle's band. None of the top white singers have ever sung on the Apollo stage.

In the way of comedians, the Apollo introduced almost every black comedian and created many stars. The ones whose names are most often connected with the Apollo are Dewey "Pigmeat" Markham, Dusty Fletcher, Sandy Burns, Johnny Lee, John "Spider Bruce" Mason, Tim "Kingfish" Moore, Spo-Dee-O-Dee, and Johnny Baskette, who later won an Academy Award as Uncle Remus in Walt Disney's Song of the South. It was essential that the funnymen who played the Apollo have a successful run—bookings at all other theaters and clubs across the country counted on it. If you made good at the Apollo, you were in.

As the TOBA Circuit began to fade, an Apollo Circuit of sorts opened up. Though it wasn't really a circuit, per se, and could not definitely be identified with the Apollo Theatre, it was all that was left. It was half a circuit—playing houses that showed movies and also had a stage show between movies. The movies were something less than B pictures, which gives you some idea of their quality; but the houses always tried to book movies that had at least one black in the cast. The typical Apollo Circuit bill would have Duke Ellington onstage and in person, and Mantam Moreland costarring in some Charlie Chan film.

By the 1950s, television began to kill off stage shows the way it had radio. Performers found they could make more money in one shot before a TV camera than they could for a whole week's work at the Apollo. Who needed the Apollo? Many of the artists who had made it big there

APOLLO THEATRE

were finding their memories a little short when it came to helping the theater that had helped put them where they were. Blinded by the big money and even bigger audiences of television, they turned their backs on Schiffman when he needed them the most.

One comedian, who had begged Frank Schiffman for work when the Toby was on the skids and had been given it, turned Schiffman down cold when the white impresario asked him to help keep his theater from collapsing by performing, saying: "Hey, bossman, I'ze sure youse heard Lincoln done freed us slaves; so why the fuck should I help you—a white man? It's our turn to turn everything around!" That attitude may have been "in," but it sure turned a lot of young black comics out on the streets who could have had a chance for stardom just as that comedian had had.

By 1971, there were only two houses left in all of New York City that supported live stage shows: Radio City Music Hall, which was really suffering because of its large capacity (5,000 seats), and the Apollo Theatre.

Others didn't forget the "home" that had given them their first chance at the big time. Nipsey Russell came back, as did Billy Eckstine. In fact, with Mr. B, it worked both ways—he won the amateur night and got his start up the ladder to superstardom. When he hit the top, he came back and played before devoted fans. Then, when his career was beginning to slow and he was no longer right up there on top, he came back again—because the Apollo needed him—but this time he was a bit unsure if the audience would accept him. To his surprise and relief, they gave him a real warm Apollo welcome and cheered after his first number. He was no longer uptight at the Apollo—and he has returned every year since.

The Apollo has spanned many eras—from the early thirties through the swinging forties of the big-band era, into the jazz-oriented fifties, the rock group sixties, and into the vocal groups of the amplified seventies. Just as music can trace black show biz history, so can comedy—

APOLLO THEATRE

from vaudeville sketches done in blackface in the thirties and forties, to straight comedians without their blackface but with outlandish costumes of the forties and fifties. Then came the standup comedians who looked straight at the audience and talked directly to them—from then on, only the subject matter and antics changed with the times.

Blackface cork died hard. It took a long time for it to be completely stamped out. The NAACP finally put its foot down and insisted that the comedians get it together and stop acting the nigger. Frank Schiffman, one of the most liberal-minded whites in Harlem, had fought against black-face for years, but without success. It took the NAACP to finally bring a halt to the useless practice of blacking up blacks. But even they had a difficult time convincing everyone. One comic who had always done his comedy under blackface was very uptight about going out onstage without his makeup. He claimed to have felt "nekid" without his cork. But eventually cork disappeared, as did the coon image.

The Apollo also introduced a new kind of entertainer to the world of show business and started something that carried over into white show biz as well. That new type of entertainer was the master of ceremonies (m.c. or emcee). Not that the emcee was new to white show business; they had been using an emcee for years. But the white emcee was either a very limited comic or merely an announcer who just introduced the acts. The performers at the Apollo, however, brought a new dimension to emceeing—they were well-rounded entertainers who could sing well, dance well, and do comedy equally well. Some Apollo emcees who rose to fame are Leonard Reed, Ralph Cooper, Nipsey Russell, and Willie Bryant. Bryant, an extremely versatile performer, formed his own band in later years and even became an actor, appearing with Ethel Waters in Mamba's Daughter.

This new breed of entertainer, the emcee, was the first to walk out onstage and talk directly to the audience—thus paving the way for other comedians to do their own

APOLLO THEATRE

thing. Some were also fine actors who employed comedy. One of these was Dusty Fletcher, who used a drunk act as his vehicle. He would wander out onstage in baggy pants, floppy shoes, battered top hat, and blackface, and a step-ladder as his only prop. Apparently drunk, he would try to climb the ladder without leaning it against anything. He'd get up a rung or two and fall off, finally calling for Richard to open the door when he fell on his face. He later recorded his now-famous song, "Open de Door, Richard," which was written by John "Spider Bruce" Mason, another blackface comedian who worked with a blackface partner called Crackshot.

Another comedian who was an actor was Johnny Lee. After a long career as a blackface comedian, he turned to acting and eventually starred as Lawyer Calhoun on the television series "Amos 'n' Andy." He got the part through a quirk of fate that often makes performers' paths cross. Some years before, Johnny had worked with Flournoy Miller as a replacement for Miller's late partner Lyles during a revival show. Flournoy never forgot Johnny's cooperation and his keen ability to read comedy lines. So, when Flournoy became head writer for the TV version of "Amos 'n' Andy," he recommended that Johnny be cast as Calhoun.

Another first the Apollo introduced to its loyal audience was the comedienne. The one who springs immediately to mind—who was Apollo's first woman comic—is the greatest of them all, the late Jackie "Moms" Mabley. She started her career earning $85 a week for 30 back-breaking shows. She finished her career bringing in well over $8,500 for just one appearance on TV.

Also a graduate of the Apollo was Eddie Green, who went on to costar on one of radio's biggest hits, "Duffy's Tavern." The list of comedians who have come out of the Apollo Theatre could fill a book, but none can compare with Dewey "Pigmeat" Markham, the comedy king of the Apollo Theatre and the audiences' all-time favorite.

John Mason in a Comedy Skit with Vivian Harris

TIMMIE ROGERS

TIMMIE ROGERS

With the phasing out of the blackface comedian, the new comedian began appearing on the stage as himself. For the first time, black comedians began to stand and talk to the audiences. Among these pioneer comedians was Timmie Rogers, who, during the forties, was half of a dance act called Timmie and Freddie. The team wore loud-colored jackets and pegged pants—the zoot-suit look.

Timmie felt that the times were right for the black comedian and that comedy acts could combine comedy with dancing. At that point, however, no one could step out alone as just a comedian.

Sid Kuller, a West Coast writer, had put together the show "Jump for Joy," which starred Duke Ellington. In this show he wrote a routine for the team of Pots, Pans, and Skillet. The routine was called "The Zoot Suit." It was the hit of the show. The influence of "Jump for Joy" had every black dude going for this new kind of drape.

Get out your tape, and measure me for a drape.
Wanna peg leg, with a reet pleat.

This was the rage of the 1940s. Sid Kuller became a household name among black performers and about that time, he wrote Timmie Roger's first act. As Timmie said himself, "I knew the time had come when a black comedian could be accepted by an audience other than the black one. There was no reason why they couldn't be as successful as white comedians who were on the scene at the time."

Prior to this, there was very little he could base his theory on. There was a smattering of comedians who worked as singles, but they had to stay in the black clubs. One of these was Allan Drew, who was labeled the black Milton Berle. He stayed a long time at the Club DeLisa in Chicago. He was known for his cigar and did one-liners in rapid-fire succession, like Henny Youngman. His material was considered blue; he was the first in a line of black

Timmie Rogers

comedians who did off-color jokes. Allen Drew played every major black club from New York to Chicago, including the Baby Grand and the Town Hall in New York. But he was never booked to play for a white audience. Comedians argue today that if Allen Drew could have played before the same audiences as Berle or Youngman, he would have been as successful as either one of them.

So Timmie Rogers decided to give it a try. He took off his green zoot suit and replaced it with a tuxedo. Timmie became the first black comedian to walk on the stage in a tux and flash all thirty-two of his big teeth. His "Oh, yeah" became a trademark and everybody accepted him.

His approach to comedy was still based on a song opening his act. His was a musical-comedy act. He did songs specially written for him.

In 1944 Timmie opened at the Orpheum Theatre with the great Nat King Cole, and that marked a new day for black comedy in America. It was the end of the comedian wearing a mask. At long last, the comic could be himself.

In those days white comedians used a catchphrase. Joey Penner always asked the question: "Wanna buy a duck?" This was a form of identification. Today Jimmie "J.J." Walker, on the television show "Good Times," is identified by the phrase, "Dy-no-mite!" Practically every phrase in Timmie's act had "Oh, yeah!" added to it. He sometimes used it as a saver, and it was always very effective. He became identified with that phrase. If you were to ask anyone who had caught any of his shows, they would tell you they heard him say it, and say it, and say it.

His talent was in singing, dancing, and comedy—a triple-threat guy. He co-wrote—with Sid Kuller, Flournoy Miller, and Al Fields—his one-man show called "Too Poor to Die." It opened at the Ebony Showcase Theatre in Los Angeles in 1956 and had a long, successful run.

Subsequent to that, he opened with Nat King Cole in a show called "The Big Show."

"Tim Gale of the Gale Agency asked me to help him put

TIMMIE ROGERS

the package together," says Timmie. "It had Duke Ellington, Sarah Vaughn, and Nat King Cole. It also boasted four
comedians, Stump and Stumpy, Howell and Bowser,
Patterson and Jackson, and, for the first time, a single
comedian—me."

"The Big Show" featured the biggest and the best in
black comedy. Stump and Stumpy was the team that
followed the same style as Buck and Bubbles. They
melded comedy and dancing. Stump was a very funny
fellow, a real clown. The team wore bright blue suits with
big white buttons on them. Stumpy was a scat singer and
the two of them would brighten any stage. In presentation
shows, the team of Stump and Stumpy was always a show-
stopper.

Another team that brought dignity and class to comedy
was the team of Howell and Bowser. Those two really
reeked with class. Bert Howell, who looked like a banker,
played violin and he was dignity personified. Buddy Bowser, who also had a very good voice, was six feet tall and
very good looking. This pair was instrumental in raising
the image of black comedy up another notch.

The other team on that show was Two Tons of Fun, the
team of Patterson and Jackson. They each weighed about
300 pounds apiece, and they could sing and dance. They
were very funny looking and funny, period. Patterson was
the comic of the two. He had a way of talking that sounded
like heavy breathing and he would buck those big eyes of
his and they would be a real house wrecker. They literally
always broke it up.

"That was the first time that a show merged a lot of big
talent—and I mean some of the giants around at the time,"
Timmie Rogers stated.

"The next thing I did, I went into the Elegant in Brooklyn
with my own show called 'No Time for Squares,'" he
continued. "That was in 1958. The next show was the one
Norma Miller and I were in together, Sid Kuller's second
edition of his hit 'Jump for Joy.' It had Duke Ellington,

TIMMIE ROGERS

Barbara McNair, Stump and Stumpy, Jimmie Randolph, and Norma Miller and her Jazzmen in it. The director was Nick Castle, and I was his assistant on that show. We opened in Miami in 1959 at Copa City.

"I was the first comedian to star in my own show at the Apollo in New York," Timmie went on. "I had with me on that show Austin Powell's Cats and the Fiddle, Buck of Buck and Bubbles, The Chocolateers; and my special guest was that wonderful singer, the late Roy Hamilton."

Timmie was recently featured on the television show "Sanford and Son," and was introduced as a new character, Smiley.

He has appeared with Sammy Davis, Jr., at the Coconut Grove in Los Angeles; he has opened Redd Foxx's show at the Thunderbird in Las Vegas; and he's now preparing his new one-man show for a future date.

Without a doubt, Timmie Rogers is a contributing talent to black comedy, and all comedians owe him a vote of thanks. As Redd Foxx tells it, "He took us out of the funny suit and put us in tuxedos."

Slappy White, who was appearing at The Village Gate in New York, once said to his assistant who came on stage in an orange suit, "I remember when we wore suits like that."

Today Timmie appears with some of the biggest stars on the scene. Redd Foxx has encouraged him to play his tippa more—that's a six-string uke. He composes many of his songs on his tippa, including two songs that Nat King Cole recorded, "It's Crazy but I'm in Love" and "If You Can't Smile and Say Yes, Don't Cry and Say No." Two other tunes of Timmie's that hit were: "Everybody Wants to Go to Heaven, But Nobody Wants to Die" and "FLA, GA, LA, PA."

BARDU ALI REMEMBERS

BARDU ALI

Although Bardu Ali isn't black, he has been an integral part of black show business for many decades. And his contribution to black humor has been invaluable. Here he tells of his part in shaping black show biz.

I've been Redd Foxx's manager-consultant-friend-you-name-it from the start of Redd's fast climb to superstardom. I'll say this about Redd right off: some comedians are funny because they write a piece of material and work at it and become good at it; then there's the other kind of comedian that's born with that little extra something that comes up funny whatever he says—this type of comedian is Redd Foxx. He didn't have to learn to say it funny; when he said it, you laughed.

It's timing. Without it comedy has no pacing. Look at all the great comedians and you'll see that the one thing they all have in common is timing. I think it's the most important asset a comic can have.

Like Pigmeat Markham. He was another great natural. The Apollo Theatre in New York saw many a great comedian, but none compared to the popularity of Pigmeat. He reigned for years as the king of the Apollo. And through the years his bits were as famous as he was.

It was at the Apollo that he originated the character Judge Pigmeat, his most famous bit. But his most famous noncomedy bit was a dancing bit; he became the rage with his interpretation of that famous dance that started like this:

They had to have something new,
A dance to do,
Up there in Harlem.
So somebody started . . .
Truckin'!

And he did. He would hunch his shoulders over, close his eyes tight, and would crunch forward to the tune of "Christopher Columbus." The people would go wild. They'd

BARDU ALI

make him do it over and over again. He was a sensation in Harlem truckin'.

At the Apollo, Pigmeat always worked with straight man George Wiltshire. Also, he always had a lady assistant, one of the most famous of which was Vivian Harris. Their bits became a landmark for the Apollo.

In his Judge Pigmeat bit, the scene would open in a courtroom with George Wiltshire announcing to the spectators: "Hear ye, hear ye! Court's in session. All rise 'cause here come de judge . . . Judge Pigmeat!"

Now Pigmeat would enter, assuming a very important look in his long black judge's robe, wearing a cardboard hat with the tassel hanging in front of his face, and carrying a telephone book. Get the picture?

Another thing he would carry as part of his standard equipment was a pig's bladder that he would have blown up like a balloon. He used this as a gavel, and whenever a defendant answered and Pigmeat didn't like the answer given, he would hit the prosecutor over the head with the bladder.

His opening remark to the courtroom after first entering from his chambers was: "Yes, I'm here, and I'm giving away a lot of time today!" Then he'd roll his eyes at the first defendant to walk up to the stand, almost always a super-sexy chick wearing a skintight dress.

It wasn't till 1943 that I was able to finally get Pigmeat to come to California, and I did it under very unusual circumstances. I was very familiar with the Apollo, as I was born and raised in Harlem, even though I'm of Indian descent, not black. And I also fronted Chick Webb's band at the Savoy Ballroom for many years and played the Toby Circuit as a dancer, as well.

So, in 1943, when I went west to visit my friend Jimmie Marshall, who at the time was manager of the Lincoln Theater in Los Angeles, I saw the Lincoln as a possible West Coast Apollo Theatre. And I got Jimmie to introduce me to the owners of the place.

There were two owners of the Lincoln: Dewey Ringer

Dewey "Pigmeat" Markham and Jimmy Baskette

(Crackshot) Hackly

Bardu Ali with Redd Foxx

George Wiltshire with Bill Robinson (left)

and Harry Popkin. I told them my idea and it was immediately rejected. "No way!" they told me. The theater was a white elephant, and they had no interest whatsoever in putting a dime into it. At the time, their only attraction was second-run pictures. I even told them I could get Pigmeat Markham and Jimmie Baskette to play the place, but they still wouldn't buy it.

I went down to the theater every day for a month until they just got tired of my coming down there and bugging them. Finally, they broke down.

"Look, Bardu, tell you what we'll do for you. We'll give you $10,000 for one week. If you make it, you got a deal. If not, don't come back. Agreed?"

I agreed.

Now, the deal was made with the understanding that I would get Pigmeat and Jimmie Baskette to play the Lincoln, but they threw me a curve—they were only willing to pay one-way transportation. I knew the only way I was ever going to get Pigmeat and Jimmie to come was to tell them that they had a sixteen-week guarantee plus round-trip transportation.

How I was going to get this deal together was a problem. So I thought about it a while and finally told Popkin to give me a contract that I could draw up for Pigmeat and Jimmie —and that I would pay the other part of the transportation out of my own pocket.

So I lied. I told Pigmeat I got a guarantee for sixteen weeks plus round-trip transportation. (Now I know where that famous phrase came from when they say, "That nigger can liiiiie!") I got the show together and began to rehearse the band when Pigmeat got into town. He took over the comedy and put together his own show.

When we opened in April 1943, the show was an instant smash, the biggest thing to hit Central Avenue ever— which you got to know was big, because Central Avenue was the heart of the black community in Los Angeles, the Harlem of L.A. There was no Watts in those days, and all the black acts in California converged on Central Avenue,

BARDU ALI

where the Alabam Club always swang and now the Lincoln Theater.

Like I say, it opened with a bang. It was the first time blacks came from everywhere, and now the Lincoln was the "in" spot in that part of town. Just to make sure it continued, we had an amateur night, just like at the Apollo in New York.

My scheme paid off. The Lincoln was a big success for the first time in its history. I would hate to think of what would have happened if we hadn't made it. But it was such a smash, we ran for over four years.

But the times were changing in 1943, and black people were beginning to resent the blackface on the comedians. So it was decided that Pigmeat would remove his burnt cork. This was a very important time in black comedy, and Pigmeat had never been onstage before without his cork.

So when the time finally came for him to do it, everyone assembled in Pigmeat's room and watched him do it. That first time he went onstage without his makeup, everyone was expecting something to happen. Nothing happened. The audience didn't even notice the difference. Unlike some other black comics, who were fair in color, it was just the opposite with Pigmeat; he was the same color, cork or no cork.

Although Pigmeat was one of the last comedians to remove the cork, he was not the last. The last of the comics to do so was Crackshot, the comedian who wore a diamond in his front tooth. Whenever he would open his mouth and do his loud cackle, the tooth would shine from the reflection of the lights as they hit it.

Pigmeat never did find out about his deal at the Lincoln until much later. It wasn't till late in 1976 when Pigmeat was visiting his old friend George Wiltshire in Los Angeles that he ever found out the whole truth about the original deal. We were sitting around at George's house, reminiscing about the old days of the Lincoln Theater, and I confessed the truth. Everybody got a good laugh over it.

During those four years we played the Lincoln, we

played all the comics. Business was great. We did one show a night and two on Saturdays and Sundays. And, of course, amateur night became a very big asset to the show. Everybody came out for amateur night.

Well, anyway, Pigmeat became very popular with the people in Los Angeles. He was the king of Central Avenue. His words and phrases were always repeated by the kids. Like his expression "Don't start no mess" caught on big.

It was while he was at the Lincoln Theater that Pigmeat was hired as a regular on the Andrew Sisters' radio show. He played the role of Alamo and was very popular doing that character.

But Pigmeat was in every phase of show business—from the Toby to television. And with Sammy Davis doing the TV show "Laugh-In" in the late sixties, when he did his "Here come de judge" routine, Pigmeat Markham was new again.

Sammy later brought him to the Sands Casino in Las Vegas and introduced him as his special guest. Pigmeat never forgot it.

And like Sammy said, there were guys in the business who walked onstage and at no time did they talk to the audience. They would be in their act as they came onstage. They did those bits the same way every time they did them; when they had to cut something from their act, they couldn't.

But Pigmeat made an important contribution to black comedy; he was amongst the best of an era. His baggy pants and funny shoes and that hat on his head all were his stock-in-trade. They will always be a part of this, our industry. He was naturally funny. He lived his entire life as a comedian. He toured all the South on one-nighters. He made hundreds of records. But he never really became a white act. His comedy stayed in the black neighborhoods and for black audiences only. There was no black audience who didn't know Pigmeat. The white audience only saw him when Ed Sullivan presented him on his TV show. He appeared on it many times and always as Judge Pigmeat.

Dewey "Pigmeat" Markham

He was Harlem's own and they loved him. Laughter was his name and comedy his game. And he was good at it.

He was also a good friend of the only black woman comic around at that time, Jackie "Moms" Mabley. They recorded around the same time and both became big through their records.

SCATMAN
CROTHERS

SCATMAN CROTHERS

Scatman Crothers—musician, singer, actor, comedian—has covered practically every facet of show business. He started out as a drummer in his own band. He acquired his name from a radio show that he was singing on in Dayton, Ohio. As he tells it:

In 1932 I went to a radio station, WBMX in Dayton, and asked to see the program director. I was introduced to Barbara Runyon. I auditioned for her and she asked me what should they call me. At the time I was using my real name, Sherman Crothers. They didn't think the name was appropriate, so I suggested they call me Scatman; then I began scatting. It was a style of singing that was very popular in those days. Remember Johnny "Scat" Davis? He was big in those days, too, from scatting.

I came out to the West Coast in 1944 with a five-piece band and it was the first bebop band on the coast. We had a lot of small clubs on the coast in those days and I got a lot of work entertaining, singing and playing. I went into the Club Oasis as a singer who walked around and sang to the customers. I worked there for four years. It was a segregated club. There was nothing black in there but me.

But times were beginning to change and a few clubs were dropping their segregated policies. I suggested to the owner at the time, "Why don't you change to a black and tan?" It was the term in those days to say black and tan; it meant both white and black could come. The management took my suggestion and it became a black and tan club.

While I was working there as entertainer and emcee, I met Redd Foxx. He was booked into the club as a comic. We became friends and have been friends ever since.

I also did one of the earlier shows on television in 1948. There was a television show that starred Dick Lane. The name of the show was "Showboat." Dick Lane played the captain and I was his sidekick. This was a typical Stepin Fetchit-type role, with me making wisecracks to the skipper. I would use phrases like, "Hey, Cap'n." I called him all

SCATMAN CROTHERS

kinds of crazy names and it got a lot of laughs. But it did get me started in television.

I'm sixty-seven years old and I've been in show business over forty years. I've been in every phase of show business. I did my first big movie in 1950. I appeared in <u>Meet Me at the Fair</u> and it starred Dan Dailey, Diana Lynn, and Scatman Crothers.

That was my first big movie. I got third billing. I knew I was going to be an actor in movies. That's why I stayed around California. That was the reason Redd stayed here, too. He said when he saw the snow on the television in December and here we were in California playing golf, he wasn't thinking about ever going back East. And you know, I wasn't thinking of going back to Dayton.

We would have some big laughs on the golf course. I'm not going to tell you what we shoot, but let's say that if Redd wasn't going to be the world's funniest comic, he could easily be the world's funniest golfer. As he says, he didn't need a golf handicap, he already had one being black.

It was tough in those days for a black comic because there was no place to work other than the small clubs that were all black. I was one of the first dudes that played white clubs. When I first went into the Club Oasis, there were no blacks nowhere. Los Angeles was very segregated then. They liked black entertainers, but they didn't want black patrons. Black comics in those days played strictly all-black clubs.

The next time I went into the Troubador, however, I went in as some kind of a celebrity—because of Redd. This time I was going in with a new rock band that was very popular. It was sold out every night during the entire engagement. It was the first time I'd be going on as an attraction for a fairly young audience. That's why I opened in the jailhouse outfit that I wore in <u>Coonskin</u>. Like the old saying, I have been around so long I'm new again. The kids dug the swing sound, and the music with the uke always has a swing beat,

Scatman Crothers as "Louie the Garbageman"

plus they did the scatting. But it did open up a newer and younger audience for me.

Today life has been good to me. My career is in high gear. I'm starting a new picture and they've decided to continue the series ["Chico and the Man"]. My home is happy. I take a swim every day to keep fit. I'm real happy. The good Lord has been good to me. At sixty-seven years old, I'm fairly healthy, my family is well, and we're all together. What else can a person ask for? I'm in the greatest business in the world—show business. I'm working, and regular. Thank God!

LEONARD REED

LEONARD REED

Leonard Reed and Joe Louis were a comedy team for many years. Everyone who went to see the Brown Bomber perform on a Las Vegas stage after the champ retired also saw Leonard.

But there's a lot more to Leonard's story than that. And he, being a writer, can tell it better than anyone else, which he does in the pages that follow.

I got my start in show business as a Charleston dancer. That's it. That was the only thing anyone knew me to be— Leonard Reed, the Charleston dancer. I started out in the business around 1920, which I guess makes me one of the oldest dudes around.

Even though I was the best Charleston dancer around, I could also write. I wrote my own shows and, at one time, staged them at the famed Cotton Club in New York. Also, I put together one of the best girl dancing lines that ever played at the Apollo.

The fact that I was always light-skinned opened a lot of doors for me. I got versatile. I became a standup comic in the hit show "Sweet and Hot," which played the Mayan Theater in Los Angeles. From there I went on to be the partner of Joe Louis in a comedy act which I wrote. Also, at one time I had my own band and to this day I still do some choreography for a lot of female song-and-dance acts around L.A.

The first show I had an opportunity to join was Lassie's White Minstrels. At the time all I was doing was the Charleston and, like all the white guys in the business, I blacked up to look black. (I was always whiter than most whites, anyway.)

The next thing I remember was that I hooked up with a dude and formed a team called Pen and Ink. He was so dark, his name was Inky. So I was Pen and he was Ink.

We played the carnivals in those days and he and I would be up there as boxers. The barker named us Jack Johnson and Jim Jeffries: I was Jeffries and he was John-

LEONARD REED

son. We'd go into our little boxing bit and people would crowd around. Then we'd do our Charleston. Man, we were something! Nobody ever could out-Charleston me. I come from being a professional contestant.

What I mean by that is I used to go in all the Charleston contests that was in town. I'd pay a cat fifty cents to let me go on first. That would give me time to run around the corner and get into another one while the rest of the first contest was still going on. I'd be heading for another one and get back to the first one in time to stand for first prize. Which was eating money.

But Inky could dance, too. He could tap dance barefoot. He'd be slapping his feet so hard he'd stir up the dust. But he could dance.

Some of the great comedians I remember back then were Billy King, Happy Donovan, Buzz and Harris, Buzz and Burtin, and Ed Lee and Lincoln Perry. I played the TOBA in a show with the Whitman Sisters. They had a show that was a real family show. Shows traveled by train back then and you could judge a show by the number of wardrobe trunks and props that they carried with them on the train. If a show was carrying a lot of trunks, it meant it was a big-time show.

The Toby gave a lot of great training to performers. Like when I worked with the Whitmans, that was where me and Willie got together. We were a dancing team. Willie Bryant and me had an act called Brains and Feet. He could rap and I could dance. We were together seven years.

After that I went back to staging shows, you know, putting together my own productions. I think I worked with all the stars on the Toby at one time or other. I worked with all the big blues singers, too—like Bessie, Mamie, and Clara Smith (and none of them were related). I also worked with the Whitman Sisters—Essie, Alice, and Alberta. You name them, I worked with them.

Some of the great comics I worked with were Gulfport and Brown and George Williams and Bessie Brown, which

LEONARD REED

was a man and woman team called Butterbeans and Susie. I opened the show for them as a Charleston dancer and they were glad to have me with them.

Willie and I started out as a team from 1930. We didn't play black houses but passed ourselves off as a white act. Nobody ever knew the difference. We had a valet that traveled with us and his name was Frankie. He was from Birmingham and used to do the encore for us.

I'll never forget the time when we got to Birmingham and we're playing a white house. No one ever thought of us as anything other than being white. Now this time we're playing Frankie's hometown. Willie always used very salty language offstage, and he would yell at Frankie (very affectionately, though), "Frankie, come here, you little black mother—". Frankie cut him off before he could finish the word: "Now wait a minute," he said. "I'm gonna tell you something. This is my home. If you and that half-white son-of-a-bitch, or whatever you call yourselves, don't cool it and calm down, I'm gonna tell 'em you're niggers!" Willie quickly hugged him, and said, "Oh, wait a minute, now you know we were only kidding you."

Frankie had us over a barrel. He said that when we introduced him, he wanted us to say that we had just discovered a dancer from Birmingham, and don't say "that boy" no more. "I am a dancer from Birmingham and my name is Frankie, get it?"

Frankie could dance. I would get the chair for him.

In Birmingham the roles changed. We were valeting for him on the stage. He would sit in that chair and he could dance better sitting than Willie and I could dance standing. He'd break it up, stop the show every time. Every time I think of Frankie, I laugh because he really turned the tables on me.

Willie and I stayed together until 1937. It was about that time that I began to associate with Joe Louis, the future boxing heavyweight champion of the world.

I was working in Detroit at the Club Plantation when I first got to know him. I had met him before, in 1934, but

LEONARD REED

this time he had just turned pro. Also, he had just had his first big fight, and he had won. He came to the club. It was an afternoon show, a cocktail hour. It was a white club, but the Sunday matinees were for black people, and he came in that afternoon to see the show.

I had a line of girls and emceed the show. Also, I would dance with the girls in some numbers. If I must brag a little, I was pretty sharp in those days. I would change after every act, and in the finale I'd come out in a bathrobe and say, "That's all, folks."

Anyway, I was all through with the show, and, as usual, I was changing my wardrobe between acts. Joe was impressed with the suit that I put on and he asked me where I got it made. I told him I got my clothes made in Cleveland, Ohio, and he said he wanted me to introduce him to my tailor. And he wanted to meet him the next day.

This was Sunday; so Monday a car picked us up—Joe and his girlfriend, and me and my Mary. We drove to Cleveland, and when the tailor saw me come in there with the Champ, he got so excited and made so much fuss about it that the whole neighborhood found out about it in about two minutes.

Well, before we could get out of the store, the whole Euclid Avenue was blocked up. Amazing Joe would walk down the aisle and say to the tailor, "Gimme two of those, some of these, and lotsa those." Well, when we walked out of that store, we looked like a circus. Joe had bought all of us camel-hair coats, wraparound. They were the rage then. There we were walking down the street in camel-hair coats, all looking alike. Man, we made a fabulous exit out of Cleveland!

We became very good friends through the years. And I was with him through his whole career. I think he liked me around because I was in show business, and he loved show business.

I wrote the act that we did for a special affair. Joe loved doing it. We began to get bookings after he retired from the ring. With Joe it was a lark.

LEONARD REED

(The following segment of the Leonard Reed-Joe Louis act is off a tape from Reed's personal collection, given to us by Leonard Reed himself.)

"I'm not going to be like all the other comedians who would walk out onstage and tell a joke, then run off and change suits, then introduce an act, then go and change suits again. This is it. Six more payments and this baby will be mine.

"There's only one way to buy a suit, that's on time—two dollars down and the rest when they catch me. If you run far enough and long enough, by the time they catch you, you've worn it out.

"Everywhere I've ever worked, I've always had it hard. I first had to lighten the theater, sell the tickets, pick up the tickets, run backstage, pull the curtain, turn on the lights, direct the band, conduct the show, go out in front and bid goodnight to the people, then put on my uniform and clean up the place, then put on my nightcap and watch it and start all over again. This is the greatest and easiest thing I've ever done in my life. Ladies and gentlemen, all I have to say is may I introduce the world's greatest fighter, the former heavyweight champion of the world, Joe Louis!"

> JOE: Well, thank you very much ladies and gentlemen. You're wonderful, Leonard.
> LEONARD: How did you like that? When you walked out on that stage, did you hear all that applause?
> JOE: I sure did.
> LEONARD: How do you like show business?
> JOE: How do I like show business? When is payday?
> LEONARD: Joe, payday isn't until Thursday.
> JOE: I'll tell you then.

Leonard Reed and Joe Louis

LEONARD REED

LEONARD: You talk like a man that's worried about his income tax or Uncle Sam or somethin'.

JOE: No, not anymore. I let Uncle Sam worry 'bout me.

LEONARD: I don't blame you, Joe. You look like you don't worry. You look healthy, but you're in a rough business now.

JOE: What do you mean, rough?

LEONARD: A highly competitive field. This is not like fighting, you know.

JOE: Not like fighting?

LEONARD: No, there's a lot of difference.

JOE: There's no difference in fighting.

LEONARD: Look out there . . . you see a lot of people?

JOE: I sure do.

LEONARD: That's the difference. In the ring, you only see one man. When you have to duck here, you have to duck many things.

JOE: What do you mean?

LEONARD: Well, you gotta be good. You gotta be a champion in this field, too, you know.

JOE: Yeah.

LEONARD: Yeah, you gotta be good. You gotta do a lot of things.

JOE: Like what, for instance?

LEONARD: Well, you know a lot of performers?

JOE: Yeah.

LEONARD: Well, you see what they do? They sing, they dance, they perform. Some of them even turn out to be movie stars, like me. You gotta learn to sing. You gotta learn to perform, Joe. You gotta be great in this business.

JOE: Well, Leonard, I could sing, and you know I know how to dance. Remember my fight with Billy Conn? I kept up with him pretty good. He led and I followed.

LEONARD REED

LEONARD: I mean really sing and dance.

JOE: That's what I mean. I could sing and dance.

LEONARD: Well, what do you think you do best?

JOE: I do them all good.

LEONARD: Okay, if you say you do them all good, let me see you dance.

JOE: You want to dance with me?

LEONARD: You want me to dance with you?

JOE: Can you keep up with me?

LEONARD: Well, a lot of guys ran from you. I guess I can keep up with you.

JOE: Okay.

LEONARD: What're you getting ready to do now?

JOE: I'm getting ready to kick the band off.

LEONARD: Kick the band off? How? One at a time?

JOE: No, all together.

LEONARD: You gonna be the leader, huh?

JOE: I'm gonna be the leader.

LEONARD: Okay, lead.

JOE: One-two-three-four . . .

(They go into a dance where Joe does nothing but egg Leonard on. Leonard does all the dancing. He finally falls to the floor, exhausted.)

JOE: What's the matter? You tired?

LEONARD: I do all the dancing and you ask me if I'm tired?

JOE: Come on, get up!

LEONARD: Get up? You didn't get up when Rocky Marciano knocked you down.

JOE: All right now.

LEONARD: I thought I'd throw that in. I thought I'd get the towel thrown in. I didn't think too much of your dancing. What else can you do?

JOE: Well, Leonard . . .

LEONARD REED

LEONARD: Don't say a word. To be or not to be, that is the question.

JOE: It is? Who said that?

LEONARD: Shakespeare.

JOE: He did? Leonard, are you sure he said that?

LEONARD: I'm positive.

JOE: Leonard, when I die and go to heaven, I'm gonna ask him.

LEONARD: Suppose he isn't in heaven?

JOE: Then you ask him.

LEONARD: Do you know any more funny jokes?

JOE: I know a lot of funny jokes.

LEONARD: Then you'd better tell one—right now.

JOE: Did you hear the story about the man standing on a busy corner with a loaf of bread under his arm, waiting for the cop to come by?

LEONARD: No, tell it to me.

JOE: Oh, forget it.

LEONARD: Can you act?

JOE: Can I act? Did you see my last fight?

LEONARD: No wonder I didn't recognize you. You're standing.

JOE: I like show business. I got a lot of wonderful friends in show business. But you know what I'm gonna do? I think I'm gonna make a comeback.

LEONARD: Don't do it, Joe. Don't do it. Please don't do it.

JOE: Why?

LEONARD: They got young guys out there today. They can move. You can't just stand there and stalk your opponent no more. You gotta move. You gotta dance around. I can hit you from any place.

(Leonard begins to dance around.)

LEONARD REED

JOE: Were you a club fighter?

LEONARD: Yeh, I fought with clubs, bats, or anything I could get my hands on.

JOE: I never heard of Leonard Reed in the fight game.

LEONARD: That was because I didn't fight under the name of Leonard Reed. That was an alias. My fight name was "Bearcat."

JOE: What was your last fight?

LEONARD: There was millions of people at my last fight.

JOE: How many?

LEONARD: There was hundreds and hundreds of people.

JOE: How many?

LEONARD: Well, somebody was in there. But Joe, what you should do today is manage a fighter— somebody like me.

JOE: Like you! You aren't a fighter.

LEONARD: I could make a comeback.

JOE: A comeback! Where have you been?

LEONARD: You should say what have I been doing.

JOE: Okay, what have you been doing?

LEONARD: I told you. I have been in training—to make a comeback. You never heard of "the Bearcat"?

JOE: I never heard of you.

LEONARD: You never heard of "Bearcat Reed, the Horizontal Kid"?

JOE: I never heard of you.

LEONARD: I have been on the floor so many times, I sold advertising space on the bottom of my shoes.

JOE: You've got to be kidding.

LEONARD: I can remember my first fight, and that's more than you can remember about your last fight. I remember when I was fighting

Leonard Reed and Joe Louis

the main event. I came out of my dressing
room. Down the aisle, moving and weav-
ing, shadow boxing in the wind. I was throwing punches in the wind. Nobody but me
and the wind. When I got halfway down to
the ring, the entire stadium stood up and
cheered.

JOE: Why? What happened?

LEONARD: I had forgotten my trunks.

THE
CONTEMPORARIES

THE CONTEMPORARIES

We have traced the changing patterns of the black comedian. We have seen him develop from his days of bondage, when his keepers would laugh at him almost automatically, to the era of the minstrelsy and later vaudeville, when blackface and an attitude of innocence and ignorance were a necessary part of an entertainer's act.

But this was to change when, in 1950, a still newer breed of comedian emerged on the scene. He was the standup comedian. He would come on the stage and stand before the audience and make them laugh just being himself. No gimmicks, no funny hats, no clown suits. There he was, looking like any other dude off the street and making people laugh.

Comedy had changed, too. Gone were the blackouts of the Apollo Theatre; gone, the situation comedy that required a straight man or an assistant. The comedian of the time was an intellectual, a philosopher, a ranconteur, a witty and articulate type of personality.

Black comedians no longer gave off the image of illiteracy. They abandoned the black dialect. The comedian that was emerging during this period, black or white, was a dude who could rap along any lines, from politics to the bedroom. He was beginning to use material with some universal substance to it, and comedy was beginning to take on a social consciousness.

But black comics still had the problem of crossing over to white houses. The comedy by black comedians was still basically working to and for black audiences.

Even so, the standup comedian had arrived and the first such comics to come down the pike were Timmie Rogers, Leonard Reed, Slappy White, and Redd Foxx. Slappy and Redd had been a team in the late forties and early fifties, working the black nightclubs. Later, each went his own way. Slappy worked the eastern part of the country, and Redd stayed out on the West Coast and began his career in Los Angeles.

THE CONTEMPORARIES

The beginning black comedians emerged nationally via the comedy album. Jackie "Moms" Mabley, the only woman among these guys, was the matriarch of comedy. She had a big influence on Slappy and Redd. She gave them the faith they needed to keep on plugging for the things they believed in. For Moms, it was very late in life before the public began to know her.

She was in her late sixties when she became a favorite on national television—mainly via appearance on the variety talk shows. Only then did her records begin to sell all over the country. And, at the same time, her toothless housewife look—with her funny little hat perched on her head and her funky old shoes worn on the wrong feet—became a national trademark. She would always say, wearing that big toothless grin of hers as she held up an apple, "I may not be able to bite 'em, but I bet I could gum 'em to death."

The mood of the people was changing, too. Organizations such as the NAACP were beginning to be concerned with the image of the black people and their portrayals of blacks. They challenged the film industry to change their methods because of the stereotyped image they were giving the blacks. So it was up to the comedian to come up with fresh ideas as well.

The impact of the civil rights movement was beginning to be felt, and black leaders like Martin Luther King were emerging as voices to be reckoned with. Civil rights was always there, but suddenly it became a great national issue. Segregation was being challenged from coast to coast, and with the explosive bus-boycott issue on the rise, the black comedian began making heavy social commentary in his work.

Although Dick Gregory was well known along the black belt, it wasn't until television news gave the escalating national crisis full coverage that he became famous for presenting the public with an entirely different type of comedy.

THE CONTEMPORARIES

It was NBC's coverage of the civil rights march that first showed Dick Gregory as a serious-minded, politics-oriented comedian. He was appearing at Robert's Lounge in Chicago when the cameras pulled in close and caught him standing there looking casual with a cigarette in his hand and talking about freedom: "Freedom in Chicago, that's a joke. I had more freedom in Alabama." From that point on, he would base his routines on the happenings of the country. But he was so refreshing in his approach that the public demanded to hear more from him.

It was this change in the public's attitude, its new awareness, that put the black comedian very much in demand. The leading clubs in America began to book black comics for the first time.

Typifying the new comic who came along at that time was the late Godfrey Cambridge. He started out in the business as an actor and took up the comedy mantle as a way to break into the big time. But he had to fight just as hard to get back to acting. He made his TV debut on "The Jack Paar Show" and became an instant hit in the comedy market.

Black comedians were now talking about any subject they chose on stage. No longer did they have to fear any reprisals if something was said that was considered risqué. Redd Foxx used to say, "They won't let me get on television because I talk about sex. Well, black folks have sex, ain't nobody drawed us."

Some of the stories told during this period were very racially oriented. One of them is about the black dude driving through the South in a very fast, white-on-white Cadillac. He's spotted by the highway police and the sheriff takes after the cat in the Cadillac. The dude in the Cadillac steps down hard on the pedal and pushes his car up to 80 miles per hour. Now he sees the sheriff, in his 1934 Ford, is gaining on him. The dude just stomps down on the accelerator and pushes the Cadillac up to 100 miles per, and the sheriff just gets his Ford up to 100 and passes the Cadillac.

THE CONTEMPORARIES

The black dude is all shook up and pulls over to the side of the road. He says to the sheriff:

"I know you got me, Sheriff, but tell me, what can you have under that hood to keep up with this new Cadillac?"

Without saying a word, the sheriff answers the question by lifting up the hood of his Ford and there are three spooks under the hood, each wearing sneakers.

It wasn't until the late 1960s and the early 1970s that black comedians began to be booked into the better clubs. Up until then clubs such as the Copa and the Persian Room of the Plaza Hotel in New York and the Chez Paree and Orchid Room in Chicago rarely booked a black comedian.

The new comedians came from a better background as a general rule. They were better educated than their predecessors; they could talk about their schooldays. Bill Cosby was a graduate of Temple University. His routine on football was a hilarious one that portrayed a black athlete in a different light.

Richard Pryor, another young man who came in through the New York coffee-house The Improvisation, began to be heard from. The coffee-house circuit was now producing many of the new comedians.

From the South—Miami, Florida—came a cute little guy named Flip Wilson. He came up through the Chitlins Circuit to the Apollo Theatre.

The black comedian at long last had a broad audience. Whether black or white, he could play before them all. No longer was it a case of being restricted to just playing for one's own ethnic group. Black comedians were now playing before Jewish audiences in the Borscht Belt and to the rock audiences at concerts, fairs, theater-in-the-round.

It's not unusual today to hear four-letter words from any comedian. Words like honky, nigger, shit, and fuck are all part of today's language.

America in the early seventies began to go through all kinds of traumas after Watergate. Any coverup action had to be revealed. It appeared to be one big confessional.

THE CONTEMPORARIES

Everybody began to uncover. Attitudes were those of: "Let it all hang out" and "Tell it like it is."

Everybody is now liberated. First it was Black Liberation, then the Women's Movement, and now Gay Lib. Whole segments of the population began to mobilize into individual pockets, each with a cause to fight.

Thinking back to the late Lenny Bruce, who was the first of a breed that today is enjoying great success, makes you wonder. When you remember what happened to him because of his use of four-letter words, the inhuman way he was persecuted by the courts, he's got to be considered a modern-day martyr.

In the movies today, we hear some of the most common four-letter words in the language, but they only bring howls of laughter. No one gets uptight when they hear it anymore. Take the picture The Last Detail as an example. Jack Nicholson portrays a sailor. In the opening scene, an orderly comes into the room and tells Nicholson that the CO wants to see him. Jack looks up and says, "Tell the CO to go fuck himself." The audience breaks up. Why? Because it's the way a sailor would talk.

In today's comedy, comedians are using the language of the street. The comedian who does this best is Richard Pryor. His characterization of the dude in the street—he introduces him as the wino—is hilarious, as are his poolroom hustler and the dude in the barbershop. They're funny because they are real.

Bill Cosby's portrayal of a young boy of twelve who tells the story of getting his "first piece of P-U-S-S-Y" hits home, too. Anyone who has seen these routines will confirm their brilliance.

The comedy of the forties showed the cat in the zoot suit. He wore a long, draped coat, pegged pants, and the big hat. Comedy of the fifties took to the tuxedos—the dangling cigarette, à la Redd Foxx, Slappy White, and Dick Gregory.

The sixties saw the arrival of the black comedian with

THE CONTEMPORARIES

the natural hairdo; the Afro was in, too, and along with it came the dashiki. And the seventies brought the character in the pink suit with the purple hat—the pimp.

The new clown is today's minstrel man—shades of the old plantation days. When you stand on a corner and you see a dude coming down the street in a pink suit with a big hat with a feather in it, over a big natural, you're likely to hear someone say, "That's a funny nigger!"

Television provided the black comic with a natural transitional vehicle to take him out of nightclubs to the tube. Prior to the "Sanford and Son" series, "Amos 'n' Andy" was the first attempt to bring black comedy in situation-comedy form to TV, and it gained instantaneous acceptance. Freeman Gosden and Charles J. Correll couldn't come from radio to the television audience with their original concept because they were white. So it was necessary to recast the show with an all-black cast. Here, comedians from old-style variety show biz and leftover vaudevillians were cast in the various roles.

From the blackface era came Tim Moore, who played the role of the Kingfish. Another blackface comedian to come to "Amos 'n' Andy" was Johnny Lee, who played the lawyer Calhoun with the tremble in his voice. Another veteran performer from the vaudeville stage was Lil Randolph, who played Mama—Sapphire's mother and Kingfish's mother-in-law. These characters were real stereotypes—exactly what blacks were trying to break away from at the time.

So "Amos 'n' Andy" became a test case, and the result was to bring to an end the era of the Tom style of comedy. No longer were the black people going to live with the image that had prevailed, depicting them in every picture made up until that time as the buffoon—the lazy, out-of-work, social outcast.

The next attempt at putting on a black sitcom was a decided break with anything that even smacked of "Tom" —the television series "Barefoot in the Park," which

THE CONTEMPORARIES

starred Scoey Mitchell as the young married lawyer who had a beautiful but kooky wife, a mother-in-law, and a neighbor. Tracy Reed played his wife, Thelma Carpenter was the mother-in-law, and Nipsey Russell was the amorous landlord. For the first time, the black man was shown in a professional capacity.

Scoey personified the difference between the standup comic and the comedic actor. His portrayal of the romantic husband proved that blacks could play love scenes without upsetting anyone over them. "Barefoot in the Park" ranks among the shows that helped pave the way for the black sitcom to become a part of our show-business heritage, and Scoey Mitchlll was a vital part of the pioneering process.

Scoey's horizons, however, have broadened since "Barefoot in the Park," and he has become a well-seasoned performer in front of the camera. Today he is much more than a comedic actor. He's branched out into drama as well and generally appears more often as a straight actor than as a comedian. Besides limiting himself to appearing in only certain kinds of roles, he is also producing his own TV specials. One of his latest, "The Comedy In America (CIA) Report," which he also helped write, featured some of the best character comedians around and was a big drawing card on the rating charts.

Scoey was the beginning of a new era for black actors and comedy actors, and his contribution was the step forward. Progress for black artists will always be a part of the history of black humor.

GEORGE KIRBY

GEORGE KIRBY

George Kirby is a voice machine. His ear is so sharp that he could be in anyone's company and before you know it, he will be imitating you. It is sometimes argued that an impressionist is not a comedian, but any time a person can stand on stage and get laughs, by whatever means, that's comedy.

George started out in show business as a bartender at the Club DeLisa in Chicago. He entertained the people sitting at the bar with his impressions of the stars that played the club.

As a youngster in Chicago, George was very big for his age; so when he turned 15, he was able to get a job at the DeLisa as a busboy. He would chop the ice for the bar and set up all the paraphernalia for the bartenders. While doing so, he learned to mix drinks with a rhythmic pattern. In those days he was inspired by Dean Murphy, who at that time was the dean of the impressionists.

He didn't know that he had any particular talent, since he always felt anyone could hear a voice and imitate it. In fact, the first time someone referred to him as a mimic, he thought it was something bad.

His impressions of Joe Williams, Al Hibbler, and Nat Cole were immediately standouts. He sounded so much like Joe Louis that he would telephone lady friends of Joe's and pretend he was Joe and make dates with them, just for fun.

George's Pearl Bailey impression is an all-time classic. Steve Allen once had Pearl Bailey on the panel of the TV show "To Tell the Truth," and they blindfolded the panel and had George do Pearl. They did not distinguish the difference till they removed the blindfolds. At the time, George was one of the few men who could do women's voices. But George was not just an impressionist who did only famous voices; he could do any voice.

Mike DeLisa soon began to notice that his customers were staying down at the end of the bar where George was working and decided it was better to have him onstage in

**Top: George Kirby and Mike Douglas; bottom: George Kirby
Caught in an Intense Moment**

the show rather than behind the bar entertaining the customers for free. Sammy Dyer, the producer of the shows at the DeLisa, told George to put together about seven minutes of material and he would put him in the next show.

George finally had his chance. He got a music writer to put down his music the way he wanted it, and when he finally opened in 1947, it was the first time the public had ever seen a black impressionist.

Opening with the now-famous "Call for Philip Morris!" routine, George was an overnight success. In fact, he was so sensational that they kept him at the DeLisa for the next five years.

After a stint in the army, he came back to the DeLisa and stayed another year. In 1959, when Willie Bryant coaxed him to come to New York, he opened at the 845 Club in the Bronx and stayed eight weeks. Duke Ellington picked up on him there and took him on his first tour. It was originally supposed to be a three-weeker, but it lasted four months.

As George tells it, going to rehearsal for his stint with the Duke was not the greatest. Everyone in show business knew that Duke's rehearsals were not always with a full band. "When I went into rehearsal, only six of the guys were there. My music was in bits and they had been used to playing an act all the way through. So when I opened that night, the audience was great but the band was rotten.

"I remember that night Duke came to the dressing room and told me he wanted to apologize because the piano player screwed up. 'But you're the piano player,' I said. Duke said, 'I know, that's what I meant, the piano player screwed up!'

"He called the whole band together to rehearse my act and that night me and the band and the piano player were sensational. The people went wild. I stayed with the Ellington aggregation for four months."

George writes all his own material and puts together his own music for his act. He's more than an impressionist; he

GEORGE KIRBY

is a rare breed of artist. He's the big, jolly giant. His impressions are of people we see every day. He continuously changes his act so that it's always fresh.

As he tells it, the time he wanted to get Ella Fitzgerald's voice, he put nickels in the juke box all day long and by the time he left, he was doing "Lady Be Good" perfectly and riffing along with her. He did Zazu Pitts, the comedienne who did the lazy style talk on the screen.

He can imitate anybody he hears. At one time he was doing so many people that it was suggested to him to sing in his own voice for a change. At first he was very reluctant, but then he finally got around to making an album, singing like George Kirby. It was called The Real George Kirby and it was a wonderful album.

In 1956 at the Beachcomber in Miami Beach, The Cotton Club Revue opened with George Kirby in the comedy spot. He was so sensational that he stopped the show cold every performance. It was his Pearl Bailey that did it.

The opening of the Cotton Club show that year starred Cab Calloway and featured the sultry singer Sally Blair. Lonnie Satin and George Kirby were also on the bill. At the time, segregation was a way of life in the South. This was the first time an all-black show had come to the beach. There was no way of knowing what the results were going to be and the producers, Benny Davis and Murray Weinger, took a wait-and-see attitude.

It was during the final rehearsals that the Miami Sun carried a headline that had everyone in the show very nervous: "We Don't Want Niggers on the Beach!" It was front-page stuff. At no time could blacks go into a new place without anxiety, and this was a typical example.

After rehearsal one night, the cast were all in their respective dressing rooms, when all of a sudden a mob was outside. Voices were heard saying, "Let's get dem niggers!"

Pandemonium broke out. Doors began to fly open, people spilled out into the halls—it was a mad scene. Then,

GEORGE KIRBY

suddenly, there was laughter. It was George Kirby, doing his voice thing.

He was more than an impressionist that night. The entire cast had a good laugh. They went on that night, relieved of their tensions, and the show was a smash. Of course, George Kirby stopped the show and continued to do so for the sixteen weeks in Miami.

Charlie Carpenter, George's friend and manager, and he are a very close twosome. Charlie has guided George's career since his days in the Cotton Club show. Today George plays all the top big rooms in Las Vegas and is a guest on all the top TV shows. His is a really class act; and he is an all-round entertainer who sings well, dances well, and tells very funny jokes. He also had his own television show that was filmed in Canada. It was on that show that he introduced his character Father Goose, where he told children's stories with a twist. He is without a doubt a major talent on the scene today, and he's always been a scene stealer in any show that he appears in.

George is the only impressionist who can do Count Basie and Duke Ellington. Actually, no one is spared. His impressions of Sammy Davis, Jr., Billy Eckstine, and Nat King Cole are gems and, of course, his pearl is that of the superb Pearl Bailey.

George Kirby is always in demand at all the top spots in show business. When he appeared in variety, he was the only comedy act on the bill. No black comedian had ever been to these spots before. He opened the doors for black comedians to be accepted everywhere. His love for show business spills over to his audience. No one who has seen George perform in clubs and on television can help but love the guy. His warmth is infectious. George sings up a storm, dances with a rotund regality, and is one of the funniest men alive. Laughter is a part of his makeup. He's a prankster, a gagster; he's always thinking up ways to make you laugh. He's a wonderful performer and a real human being. Everyone who sees George falls in love with him instantly.

NIPSEY RUSSELL

NIPSEY RUSSELL

One night in 1948 at the Baby Grand on 125th Street and Eighth Avenue in New York, a young man made his debut there with no fanfare and was instantly the talk of Harlem. That young man was Nipsey Russell.

Nipsey and the Baby Grand went together like coffee and cake; the marriage lasted twenty years. By the time Nipsey had come to New York, he was well prepared for the black houses. He had played what was left of the Toby, but when he was on it, it was already renamed the Chitlins Circuit, called that by those acts who played the remnants of a day gone by.

Nipsey is originally from Alabama, and his beginnings as an entertainer in the South in the forties were very depressing. As the times changed, so did the audiences. They demanded a more sophisticated type of comedy, and they definitely frowned on the dialect style of comedy that the South had gotten used to.

By the time Nipsey Russell reached New York, there was no trace of a southern accent in his speech. He spoke very articulately. His poems were a part of his act even then. He was one of the first comedians to keep a comedy file on material. Nipsey wrote material for every occasion, and at no time was he ever caught off guard when onstage.

No one handled the Baby Grand audience better than Nipsey Russell. The policy of the Baby Grand was two shows a night, and Nipsey, who served as emcee-host and comedian, was able to get the show going every night and do his own act as well.

Nipsey was one of those comedians who came from emceeing to being a standup comedian on his own. Two comedians who worked this way in those days were Leonard Reed and Ralph Cooper, and Nipsey followed them into the Apollo Theatre as emcee and comedian. It was at the Apollo Theatre that he was named "Harlem's Son of Fun." In front of a black audience, he knew his job.

Some of Nipsey's earlier boosters included Billy Eckstine and Sammy Davis, Jr. As Sammy tells it, "Nipsey was

Nipsey Russell

NIPSEY RUSSELL

a very funny fellow. I went to him when I started to do lines in my act and Nipsey gave me the lines that got me started. Nipsey had never played out of Harlem; so when I was going into Robert's Lounge in Chicago, I asked Nipsey to go with me. He was so surprised. I knew he would be great. All he needed was the chance."

Nipsey got his first television exposure through Jack Paar, when the latter hosted "The Tonight Show" on NBC. Nipsey was so well liked by Paar that he was booked many times after that. His ability to come up with a poem for any occasion makes him a favorite on any television show. He's called the "Poet Laureate of Comedy."

His image was that of the first black comedian to have the intelligence to work with a script. His material was always well thought out, and at the mike he did not have the presence of your typical coon—loud laughter, funny clothes, and so on. Nipsey needed no gimmicks or characterizations; he just stood there and talked. Although some of his lines were in rhyme, most of the time he could get his audiences to laugh by just being himself. Television audiences (black and otherwise) got to know him, so they weren't shook up when he appeared as Nipsey Russell.

The first time his concept was tested was in 1964, when Nipsey was booked at the Catskill's Concord Hotel in Monticello, New York. Philly Greenwald was the first of the buyers to book a black comedian. When Nipsey appeared at the Concord, it was with Cab Calloway starring, Norma Miller and her Jazzmen opening the bill, and Nipsey in the comedy spot. Of course, it was still a black show playing the Borscht Belt, but it was an entire ethnic house, mostly Jewish. They loved Cab, who was always a favorite; and a dance act is always an important part of a black show. But the thing that was different was that, for the first time, they were hearing a black comedian trying to relate to a Jewish audience. With a comic of Nipsey's calibre, there was no problem. Of course, Nipsey didn't like the idea of his being with a black show, and on the first time out, he voiced his

NIPSEY RUSSELL

disapproval: "I didn't leave the Baby Grand to be part of a Cotton Club show," he complained. As did all other black performers, Nipsey resented being forced into the white man's mold. Playing before an all-white audience was an accomplishment; playing the comedy spot as himself instead of as some stereotyped black character to satisfy his audience was, too. But as long as he was playing with all black entertainers, he might as well be playing for black audiences—he hadn't made a step forward; he had made a step sideways so far as he was concerned.

Nipsey is another one of those brilliant entertainers who changed the picture of the black comedian and paved the way for others to break from the mold. He is a much sought-after panelist for almost every game show on TV, where his clever and appropriate poems and ready wit amuse and delight the viewers. When he isn't convulsing studio audiences with his one-liners or helping contestants win great sums of money, he's playing the top casinos in Las Vegas.

He is a monologist, and he has come a long way—from the Toby Circuit and the Baby Grand to Vegas and national TV. And his many years at the Harlem nightclub prepared him well for the career that was yet to come. He is today, without a doubt, the finest of his special breed of comics. His work is always well put together and his joke file is loaded with every type of material that could possibly be written.

While Nipsey was appearing at the Baby Grand, other comedians were beginning to emerge. The country was going through a civil rights crisis and the comedy of the day reflected it in the clubs and the few theaters that were open to live shows.

Nipsey began using the line, "The natives are restless," which became very popular in its day. The bus boycott in Montgomery, Alabama, had a direct effect on comedy, especially with such comedians as Nipsey, himself a product of Alabama. He followed the events closely, of course,

NIPSEY RUSSELL

and his material began to take on a different tone—a civil rights tone. Nipsey was perhaps more influential in this new type of comedy than almost anyone else because he was making frequent appearances on "The Tonight Show" with Jack Paar. Here's one tale he told on that show:

"The African delegate was driving on Highway One, between Baltimore and Washington, D.C., and stops at this restaurant to dine. When he enters, he's told that blacks can't be served there. The delegate, all flustered with embarrassment, pulls up all his dignity and says in a very loud voice that he was the African delegate from Ghana. The waitress looks him straight in the eye and says in just as loud a voice, "Well, you ain't Ghana eat here!"

Nipsey Russell was also responsible for some of the more memorable gags that came out of that dismal period of history when the civil rights leaders were trying to get right-to-vote privileges for blacks.

For instance, he told one about the citizen who approached the registrar's office to vote for the first time and was asked many questions:

Q: Who was the first president of the United States?
A: The first president was George Washington.
Q: Who were the signers of the Declaration of Independence?
A: How should I know? Y'all didn't tell me yet.
Q: What did the Founding Fathers mean when they said all men were created equal?
A: They meant when you're white, you're right; when you're brown, you could stick around; but when you're black, get waaaaaay back!

The tone of the comedy was biting in its revelation of how deep the prejudice went.

Another of Nipsey's gags was about the black man leaving the South because of all the unrest. As he sits in the

NIPSEY RUSSELL

bus station waiting to catch a bus going north to Chicago, he notices a scale that tells your fortune as well as your weight on a little card that shoots out. He goes up to the scale, steps on it, and drops a coin in the slot. A little card comes out that reads, "You weigh 150 lb., you are a Negro, and you're on your way to Chicago." This so surprises the man who's just been identified as a Negro that he finds it amazing. So to be sure, he tries it again. And again, the card comes out and reads, "You weigh 150 lb., you are a Negro, and you are on your way to Chicago." By this time, he's all shook up with disbelief.

So this time he spies an old Indian sitting all wrapped up in a blanket. He approaches the Indian, borrows his blanket, and proceeds to wrap it around himself as a disguise. He sticks a feather in his hair and slithers up to the scale, deposits another coin, and another little card shoots out. It reads, "You still weigh 150 lb., you're still a nigger, and by fucking around, you've missed your bus to Chicago."

SLAPPY WHITE

SLAPPY WHITE

Melvin "Slappy" White began his career in show business as part of a comedy dance team called The Two Zephyrs. They wore outlandish zoot suits with oversized caps and used two big dice as their props. Also, they carried menacing razors.

At one time Slappy was teamed with the late funny guy Willie Lewis. Later he teamed with Redd Foxx, where they developed a very funny stage entrance.

Foxx would enter and say, "I'm Foxx." Then Slappy would enter and say, "I'm White," which would bring a surprised look to Foxx's face. He would then say, "You're kidding." And Slappy would reply, "No, I'm not kidding. I'm White and I'm your lawyer." Then Redd would say, "Oh, well, start lawyering then."

With the breakup of the partnership of Foxx and White, they each went on to separate careers. Slappy's first big show as a single, a standup comedian, was in 1957 at the Cotton Club in Miami Beach. This was the second season of the Cotton Club show; George Kirby starred during the first. This one had Slappy White in the comedy star role. It was Slappy's first time out, and the beginning was shaky. He was having a difficult time and Benny Davis, the show's producer, didn't help. He wanted Slappy to use a certain joke because of the heavily Jewish audience in the room. But the trouble was that it had an ending Slappy really didn't understand. He kept confusing the words "Man, a sheygets" (meaning: hey, a non-Jewish boy) with "Manischewitz." After rehearsals, Benny would say, "Slappy, the line is 'Man, a sheygets—man, a sheygets!'" Slappy's comeback was, "With my luck they'll be all colored people in the house."

He became the first black comic to appear at the Catskill's Concord Hotel in Monticello, New York, and following that he appeared for a period of eight seasons at the famed Club Harlem in Atlantic City in the Larry Steele's Smart Affairs Revue. It was during the time he spent at the Club Harlem that Slappy developed as a great standup comedian.

SLAPPY WHITE

In 1967 he teamed up with Steve Rossi and became a first again. Theirs was the first black and white comedy team to gain any kind of prominence. They appeared at the Americana in New York, the Coconut Grove in Los Angeles, and the Sahara Lounge in Las Vegas. They were even introduced by Ed Sullivan from the audience, and if Sullivan pointed someone out from the audience, that meant recognition.

Slappy White is a meticulous kind of comedian. Like Redd Foxx, he has influenced more comedians than most. Scoey Mitchlll admits openly that he stole Slappy White's whole act and began his comedy career with it. And there have been others who have done the same.

Many of Slappy White's stories are still the funniest. He has written jokes for Redd Foxx and a lot of material for the late Moms Mabley as well. Slappy appeared with her in Moms's last film, <u>Amazing Grace</u>. Writer Don Reo, who produces the television series "MASH," started his career in show business as Slappy White's assistant. Don's entrance onstage was in a loud orange suit and Slappy would say, "I remember when we used to dress like that."

A lot of Slappy's jokes are racially slanted. He began in comedy as segregation was first being challenged on all sides and naturally his comedy reflected it. At the closing of his act, he would always do a bit with a pair of gloves, one white and one black. He called this his Brotherhood Creed. It was requested by President Kennedy as a creed for the American soldier, and Slappy wrote it for the president.

After having the audience in hysterics for over forty minutes, Slappy would introduce his creed by saying: "Racial jokes are not going to solve the problem we have in this country. I don't tell a racial joke to offend anyone. I try to create a little humor so that all people can laugh."

He would then dig into his pockets and pull out the gloves. After putting them on, he would hold up the white glove and then the black one, moving his gloved hands expressively throughout his recitation. He would say:

SLAPPY WHITE

If the white man and the black man
Would walk hand in hand,
We could make this a wonderland.
You've got George Washington,
We've got Booker T.
You've got men in Congress,
And so do we,
We'll stop calling you ofay,
You stop calling us spades.
Together we could wipe out poverty, disease,
And we could conquer outer space.
So why don't we get together
And let all men join the human race.

At the conclusion he would clasp the white and black gloves together as a dramatic symbol of brotherhood.

Slappy White works from a set routine, and his material is planned out to the nth degree. He is what is known as a "design" comedian; he has definite lines to say when he's onstage, and he rarely strays off course.

He has a very quick mind; he's very inventive. His monologues are all on the issue of race because he was deeply involved in the early days of the civil rights movement, and his comedy reflected the times.

During the 1972 presidential campaign, Slappy developed a routine based on the press coverage of the candidates. Senator Muskie, the Democratic hopeful for the presidency, was asked to pick a black man for his second spot on the ticket. This news prompted Slappy to state, "It's better to run <u>with</u> a black man than <u>from</u> one." He wrote the routine "Slappy White for Vice-President" and campaigned in Las Vegas with campaign buttons, slogans, speeches, gags. And, oh, yes, a full-blown press conference (rigged, of course), that went like this:

As you know I'm running for the vice-presidency and any questions you want to ask the ol' vice-prez, go on and ask.

Q: Mr. White, I'm Tommy Scott, <u>Time</u> and <u>Life</u>, and

SLAPPY WHITE

we'd like to know about your running for the vice-presidency. What about Mr. Muskie? What about him?

A: Well, with him being Polish and me being black, I'll add a lot of class to the ticket.

Q: Mr. White, I'm from the NAACP, the black caucus of Capitol Hill.

A: You mind standing up, brother, so that I can see your black caucus? Oh, there you are. Do you mind dimming your teeth?

Q: Mr. White, you say that a black vice-president will help the economy. Now, how is that?'

A: Right off the bat, I'll fire the chauffeur. I'll do the driving myself.

Q: Mr. White, you say that black is beautiful?

A: Yeah, but you got to turn the light on to appreciate it.

Q: Mr. White, what do you think it will be like when you become the first black vice-president?

A: Well, I might not be black by the time I am elected.

Q: Oh, how is that?

A: Well, you know how a steak is good for a black eye? Well, I'm having a suit made out of meat.

Q: Mr. White, you say having a black vice-president will help us with the unfriendly foreign powers. Which ones?

A: The NAACP, CORE, and Nipsey Russell.

Q: Mr. White, what is meant by black power?

A: Prune juice.

Q: Then what is white power?

A: Milk of magnesia.

Q: Mr. White, what's the biggest problem for you as a black man with the second spot on the ticket?

A: Tryin' to find a white man for the first spot on the ticket.

Q: Mr. White, who first asked you to be the Democratic candidate?

A: The Republican party in Cicero, Illinois.

SLAPPY WHITE

Q: Mr. White, I understand that Howard Hughes came to your rally?

A: Yes, a big long Cadillac pulled up, a chauffeur got out and opened the door, and nobody got out. I said, "My man Howard!" He spoke to me, too.

Q: What did he say?

A: Get out of my way, nigger!

Q: I understand they gave you a testimonial dinner in Washington, D.C.

A: Yeah, it was the first time I have ever been to an inaugural dinner where they served champagne, caviar, and ham hocks.

Q: Why were you so late coming to the studio tonight?

A: I got on the wrong bus. I got on a school bus. Carried me eighty miles out of the way. I asked a little kid who was riding the bus, I said, "Man, we've gone a long way. You ride this bus every day? Where do you live?" He said, "In Las Vegas." I said, "Where do you go to school?" He said, "In San Francisco." I wouldn't let them bus me that far if it was slavery time!

Q: Mr. White, most candidates take their wives on the campaign trail with them. Why don't you take yours?

A: My wife always nags all the time. Nag, nag, nag!

Q: Oh, she's a nagger?

A: No, she's a Mexican.

Q: Mr. White, why was the black vote so low last election?

A: Well, it's hard to write with a ball-point pen . . . on wax paper . . . over butter.

Q: Mr. White, I hear that you started your campaign off as a poor man. Did you come from a poor family?

A: I was born in a log ghetto. Actually, my family was so poor, when somebody threw our dog a bone, we'd signal for a free catch. We were pooooor!

Q: Mr. White, President Nixon said that he was going to end the war on poverty.

SLAPPY WHITE

A: Yeah, he said poor people got to surrender. I joined the war on poverty last week.

Q: How was that?

A: I threw a grenade at a tramp.

Q: Mr. White, ours is a government of the people, for the people, and by the people, right?

A: Everybody but the people in Washington.

Q: Do you think China should be admitted to the United Nations?

A: Anybody who got 800 million people and claims that Ping-Pong is their indoor sport will lie about anything.

Q: Mr. Nixon said his trip to China was for the good of the country.

A: Well, if his going was good for the country, why is he coming back?

Q: Mr. White, what is the darkest part of Africa?

A: Looking up a Mau Mau's muumuu.

Q: Mr. White, do you think that being vice-president would change you?

A: No, I'd be the same guy, riding around in a Cadillac I don't own. And I got a trailer, too . . . the finance company's.

Q: Mr. White, how do you stand on the draft?

A: At the end of the line . . . on crutches . . . with a purse . . . and my slip showing. Just call me the fruit of the loom.

Q: Mr. White, where would be the best place to be in case of a nuclear attack?

A: Anywhere you can say, "What was that?"

Q: Mr. White, you say if you get elected, you'd get rid of all the dope. Is that true?

A: Friends, put me in office and I'd take all the marijuana, the cocain, the heroin, and throw it in the river! I'd take all the whiskey, wine, and beer and throw it in the river. I'd take all the bad women and throw them in the river! And when I leave here, I'm going down the river.   Goodnight folks!

DICK GREGORY

DICK GREGORY

While other comedians had broken new ground for the black humorists of today—first by doing single comedy acts, then by dropping their use of burnt cork, and finally by changing from buffoonery costumes and actions into cool cats in tuxedos—Dick Gregory did far more than all the others put together. He led the black comedian out of the stereotyped rut the whites had forced him into for so long by almost literally biting the white hands that were feeding him.

As the first black comedian to stand up in front of a white audience and say what had so often been said before black audiences, Dick Gregory made news. His timing was right on—he was performing during the civil rights crisis, and he was telling it like it was. In his tux, and without a coon characterization to hide behind, that brilliant dude let the white people see what they had been doing through their prejudice. And he made them laugh at themselves—through truth.

His comments painted some hilarious pictures: "Can you imagine how it will be, when they hire the first Negro bus driver in the South, and the steering wheel's twenty-five feet long?"

He really made the white folks stop and think, because there was so much truth in what he was saying. One of his most famous lines is: "What a country! Where else could I have to ride in the back of the bus, live in the worst neighborhoods, go to the worst schools, eat in the worst restaurants—and average $5,000 a week just talking about it?"

After a long drag on his always-present cigarette, he'd continue: "Makes you wonder. When I left St. Louis, I was making five dollars a night. Now I'm pulling in $5,000 per week—for saying the same things out loud I used to say under my breath."

Dick Gregory was born and raised in a St. Louis slum, the second of six kids. His mother would always remind her kids: "We're broke, not poor. There's a difference." Dick carried this dignity with him right up through school,

Dick Gregory

where he went four years to Southern Illinois University, distinguishing himself as a track star.

With his brilliant sense of humor, it was only natural that he should head straight for nightclubs instead of into the business world he had studied for. He made his way to Chicago and worked the Esquire Club and then Robert's Lounge in the late fifties. He was beginning to get tired of having to tell risqué jokes in small clubs when his big break came. It was the height of the civil rights crisis, and Dick was asked to substitute for a white comedian who had become ill—at the Penthouse room of the Playboy Club in Chicago. He was booked in for three weeks—and stayed for nine.

While he was there, delivering his views on segregation and the white man's treatment of the blacks, a reporter from Time magazine dropped in. He was so impressed by this intelligent, sophisticated young comedian that he went back to New York and wrote a full article on the fast-rising new comedy sensation, Dick Gregory. The Time article led to an offer to be on "The Jack Paar Show"—and Jack proudly took credit for having discovered Dick. Hugh Hefner would have disputed that. But it wasn't so important who discovered him as that America had finally discovered him.

As the first black comedian to play such a prestigious nightclub—one that most white comics would give anything to play—Dick had really swung the door open wide to all black comedians who were enterprising and inventive enough to pour through. Because he was such a smash on his many visits to "The Jack Paar Show," Dick was invited to play the very top clubs in the country. In the space of a couple of months, he had become a superstar.

After he played the hungry i in San Francisco, people on the West Coast started calling Dick the black Mort Sahl—and Mort, the white Dick Gregory. Dick would tell his audiences: "If I've said anything to upset you, maybe it's what I'm here for. Lenny Bruce shakes up the puritans;

DICK GREGORY

Mort Sahl, the conservatives; and me—almost everybody!"

Explaining how he could get away with such outrageously antiwhite material, Dick once said, "Once I get them laughing, I can say anything." And it was true. His audiences cracked up on line after line aimed at them. He barely gave them time to catch their breath. He would say: "You gotta say this for the whites—their self-confidence knows no bounds. Who else could go to a small island in the South Pacific where there's no crime, poverty, unemployment, war, or worry—and call it a 'primitive society'?"

At that time, Dick's material was not completely devoted to racial issues. He had a clever mind that didn't think along ordinary lines. A good example of his way-out thinking: "Do you realize that the calendar on your wall is called the Gregorian Calendar? You folks better be nice to me—or I won't let you use tomorrow."

Most comedians who came after him—and those who had been struggling along in black nightclubs and on black circuits for years before he made the scene—admit that they owe a lot to Dick. Not just because he opened doors for them, but because he opened whole new avenues of thought and methods of expression that the black comedian had never been allowed to tap before.

It was while Dick was performing at the hungry i that he had a clause written into his nightclub contracts that said he could leave his booking at a moment's notice if there was a demonstration or a march he was needed at anywhere in the country. At this point, he was such a smash, bringing in such huge audiences, that the club owners were happy to agree—just to be able to pack the house on the nights when he was there.

But Dick not only bit the hand that was feeding him once too often, he took too many chunks out of it. He became so wrapped up in the cause of racial equality that he began to lose sight of his humor. Soon he was spending more time out picketing and sitting in than he was performing, and the club owners were feeling the pinch.

DICK GREGORY

People didn't like to get all dressed up, hire a babysitter, drive clear downtown, pay for parking, pay a heavy cover-charge, and find that they had to see some other comedian because Dick had just taken off for a march through Mississippi or a sit-in in Washington. And when he did show up to perform, his humor had grown more and more bitter.

Dick now spends most of his time on racial equality. And he will never be forgotten as the man who shattered the racial barrier for black comedians—and black people. His most famous story will live long after we have all passed from the scene. It's the one about when he went into a restaurant in the Deep South and was told they didn't serve colored people. He answered: "That's okay, I don't eat colored people; just bring me a ham sandwich."

GODFREY CAMBRIDGE

GODFREY CAMBRIDGE

Godfrey Cambridge, who died recently while filming the television movie <u>Entebbe</u> (he played the role of Idi Amin), was both an actor and a comedian. In his many appearances on "The Jack Paar Show," he showed himself as a brilliant standup comedian. Just before he died, he did an interview with Walter Burrell on comedy. Here are some excerpts from that interview.

BURRELL: How do you choose your material?

GODFREY: When it comes to choosing material, I don't play to any specific group, especially hippie material. A comic that plays to hip groups or supposedly "in" groups is playing strictly to a minority group. And when you go to a place like Vegas and you come as a hip comic per se, you find that the only guys that are laughing are the boys in the band. It doesn't take much intelligence to figure out that the boys in the band ain't paying you.

What you do is this: you have ideas which you are trying to get across and you find a way to do so that the audience doesn't doubt what you mean, and yet they laugh. If they are laughing at a joke in Vegas, I say, "Well, they're all down from Salt Lake City tonight," and they're all familiar with the Mormon background and they identify. When I talk about alimony, it's not just black alimony, it's alimony in general.

Now there are certain facets which come into play because I'm black and they're unique, but everyone laughs because they know about alimony, divorces, et cetera. So what do I do? I take the truth and twist it. Or I take something that is untrue, as Genet did in <u>The Blacks</u>, and take it to such ridiculous proportions that you see how absurd it really is. I'll take a situation and stretch it until it cannot hold any real truth anymore. It becomes ridiculous, so I find it very difficult to find anybody to write for me.

Another thing I found out is that I no longer walk onstage to "make points," like here's one for the white people, one for the blacks, another for the Jews. I go out to have fun, to enjoy myself, to give love and to get it back.

Godfrey Cambridge

GODFREY CAMBRIDGE

There are some times I fail. There are some times when the audience fails. But I'm honest enough to know when that happens. When I'm working in a club and there are guys out there that are drunk, you've got a man who's there because his old lady said, "You're gonna take me to see Godfrey Cambridge. I'm not going back to that hotel till you take me to see him!"

So this cat hates you as soon as you walk on. Sometimes you can look in the audience and almost hear the argument which took place back at the hotel. He said, "I ain't payin' good money to go see that nigger!" And she obviously insisted, "Yes, you are!" And you know he's sitting there hating you. Finally, about midway through the act, you might get him on your side.

But I don't go out to make points and I don't go out just to do an hour and fifteen minutes. I go out like it's my living room. It's my ball game.

BURRELL: What about black comedians who trade strictly on the ethnic thing? Do you see this as limiting or do you perhaps see this as a very necessary stage in the overall comedic development?

GODFREY: I see this as limiting oneself. But it's also very often that everybody has his own statement to make. If they're black and they have a black statement to make and it's been building up inside them for years, all their lives, let them go ahead and get it out.

I've been flattered that some comics have seen fit to do some of my routines from my albums, word-for-word. I don't get uptight about it. White comics have been doing it for years. When a comedian becomes identified with a certain piece of material, nobody can really take it from him. It's like going out and doing Fat Albert or Weird Harold. You know right away it's Bill Cosby. The audience may laugh, but how much of a future would the comic have doing another's material? How long could he imitate Cosby or Kirby or Nipsey Russell or whoever?

GODFREY CAMBRIDGE

BURRELL: Speaking in that vein, did you have a particular mentor when you were a developing comedian? Is there anyone you patterned yourself after?

GODFREY: It's so strange. I patterned myself after Jack Benny and, to a certain extent, Jack Carter. But mostly Benny. And it's strange how it happened. I came from a very religious family and the only place you could see any black comedians was in the nightclubs and theaters, and my folks didn't allow me to go there. So I listened to the radio and heard Benny, Allen, and Jack Carter or whoever appeared on "The Ed Sullivan Show."

I like the idea that Benny used words and gestures economically. He'd use his hands; a raised eyebrow meant so very much, a pause at precisely the right place. So I came to pick this up and still do my own thing with it. So what I did was pattern myself after them and eventually my own self evolved. I got my little tape recorder and stole stuff from here and there, and I was a big hit at the New York Housing Authority Christmas party.

BURRELL: Of course, there was a big difference in that you were adding a whole new dimension to their material in that you were black.

GODFREY: Oh sure, it came out a different way. And it brings me back to what I said earlier—that I'm still developing and I keep my mind open to change and new ideas. A comedian in many ways is an historian. He reflects the times and the mood of the country and the world. If he didn't develop constantly, he'd become stale and die as a comic. I'm too excited about life to let that happen.

BILL COSBY

BILL COSBY

If there is such a thing as reincarnation, then Mark Twain is back among us. However, this time he came back black; he came back as Bill Cosby.

Bill Cosby was the first of the black comedians to come out of the improvisation school—the school that trains a performer to take a subject, develop it, and make it come out funny, without knowing in advance what direction he's going in.

This style became very popular during the 1960s, and Cosby was quick to master it. No one develops a routine on the spot better than he, as witness one of his early anecdotes called "Noah"—a brilliant piece of work based on the Bible story of Noah. In it he gives a humorous accounting of the tale about the animals being taken to the Ark, and the conversation Noah had with the Lord.

His work that was shown on national television called "I'm a Bigot" again displayed his great talent for making a subject amusing and, at the same time, profound.

Bill Cosby was the first black comedian to star in a weekly television series. He and Robert Culp costarred in the long-running "I Spy," where each one's role enhanced the talent of the other. It was the first time a black actor appeared with a white star and did not have a buffoon part, i.e., that of a valet, a chauffeur, or any other offshoot of the master-slave syndrome. It was a first for many doors that began to be opened up to black performers.

Cosby brought to black comedy and the image of the black comedian a dignity that prior to his coming into prominence had been unheard of. He gave the intellectual side to humor. He did not at any time play the condescending part in the two-man relationship in "I Spy." At times it was the comedian who was influencing the actor. Most actors feel they can play comedy, and when an actor works with a comedian, it's natural for the actor to try to get the laugh lines. In "I Spy," it was always Bill who was influencing Robert; you could hear the actor read the line like the comic. After the two had been working together for a time, Culp began to sound like Cosby.

BILL COSBY

A comedian is an observer and this is very true of Bill Cosby. He looks into a subject, analyzes it, and then proceeds to go in and pull it out and hold it up before us so we can all see it for what it is. Then, in the light of cold objectivity, we laugh at it.

His subjects are always those we can identify with. He lets you see that being black is no different from being white or brown or whatever color. We are all the same in our basic emotions, and that's what he likes to capitalize on.

When he talks of his family life, he's so real. We all identify with what he is saying about aunts and uncles and sisters and brothers, regardless of our different ethnic backgrounds. We find ourselves laughing at the same things.

In Las Vegas, where he appears at the Hilton, Cosby never fails to bring to his shows something different. His props consist of one big overstuffed chair placed in the center of the stage. Without music, singing, or dancing, he just sits there and talks to you, as if he were talking just to you. He holds your attention for a solid hour and you never want him to leave. He has you mesmerized. He is an in-depth performer. He goes in deep and really makes you laugh.

When his wife, Camille, had their first baby, Cosby would get up onstage and tell us what happened—about when her time came to go to the hospital and what happened when she got there. Anyone who has gone through childbirth for the first time identifies with what he says.

He did a routine on a young boy, about twelve, going out to get his first piece of "P-U-S-S-Y." It's hilarious. He tells about a group of preteen boys bragging about Rosemary and that Rosemary "got some good P-U-S-S-Y." Being young and not knowing what a "good piece of P-U-S-S-Y" was, the twelve-year-old began bragging, telling the boys he had a date with Rosemary and he was going to get a piece of "P-U-S-S-Y." So there he was that evening, calling on Rosemary and saying to himself, "Wow, man,

Top: Bill Cosby as a Young Comic; bottom: Bill Cosby in a Typical Benign Grimace

BILL COSBY

I'm going to get me some 'P-U-S-S-Y!'" When Rosemary comes to the door, he starts to get worried because he doesn't know what "P-U-S-S-Y" is. So when he finally sees Rosemary and she shows him, he says, "Now I'm really in trouble. I don't just not know what it is—I don't even know what to do with it!"

Cosby's commercials on Jello, with all the kids around him, are a joy. He makes such simple things so funny. His love for children comes right through the tube because he never talks down to kids; he talks to them and becomes one of them. He relates to them and it comes across to the viewing public, and they in turn relate to him.

He is a wonderful comedian who will always be young. He's like Peter Pan; his world is ever, ever young. His warmth touches everyone who sees him and listens to him. He is to black people what Mark Twain is to Missouri, what Walt Disney is to movies.

Bill was telling us how he began his career in Philadelphia, and at the time he had a partner. "It was Pop Foster who told me to go it alone, and I am glad that I did. At the time I came into show business, Dick Gregory had set a standard that changed comedy from where we did the funny stuff with funny clothes, and the comedy had lost the buffoon look. For the first time people could listen to a black man talking on an intellectual level. No longer did the subject matter have to be about Liza Jane. Now a dude could rap.

"I remember the first time I saw George Kirby just standing there and talking. I was so impressed that it started me off on talking without telling jokes or stories. Life itself had all the comedy you needed. When you begin to put into words the things that happen to you and everyone else, every day of their lives, it's funny. So my subject matter became the public, home, my mother, my wife, my little brother Albert, Fat Albert.

"After graduating from Temple University, and when I

BILL COSBY

went into show business, I started talking about my football days and found acceptance for what I did. That encouraged me to continue in that style. Times were changing and because Dick Gregory had such an impact on the public's mind, it was a decided influence on what the public thought of me. Comedy was now going into the dignified vein. I knew that I had an opportunity to help the black man in my interpretation of him."

FLIP WILSON

FLIP WILSON

Flip Wilson began in show business in Miami, having seen the last remnants of the Chitlins Circuit. He came up from Miami to New York and reached the Apollo Theatre, where he could be seen in many of the variety shows presented there on a weekly basis. Along with comedians like Redd Foxx and Slappy White, Flip also became part of that group of young comedians who helped change the look of comedy among the black audiences.

No one who saw Flip in those days could have doubted his eventual success. He was known for his ability to tell a story. But it was his antics, along with the storytelling, that the public enjoyed. When Flip tells a story, you almost wish he wouldn't end it. And he doesn't rely on monologues laced with one-liners. When he's telling a story, his phrases are emphasized with body motion, facial expressions, and funny voices. He acts out the entire story, character by character.

Another big part of his charm is his funny little way of breaking up when he's said something either very cute or very provocative; it's vital to his whole presentation. In the beginning, his characters were only voices, but with the television cameras on that impish face of his, the characters became bigger than life. Now many of his characters have a life of their own, and his Geraldine is nearly as famous as he is.

When Redd Foxx was appearing on "The Tonight Show," and host Johnny Carson asked Redd, "Who do you think are the new comedians on the horizon?" Redd immediately answered, "Flip Wilson." It was then and there that Carson decided to get Flip for a guest shot. He'd already been seen on "The Ed Sullivan Show," and there was no doubt about it, Flip Wilson was coming up fast.

He became the first black comedian to host and star in his own weekly variety series on NBC. It was television that brought his famous characters to life, like preacher Reverend LeRoy, and, of course, the all-time great character Geraldine.

FLIP WILSON

Reverend LeRoy was always a very popular character on the stage and in the nightclubs, but this was during a period when black clergymen were going through some heavy changes. They put up a squawk about his takeoffs on the southern ministers.

Flip decided to soft-pedal the Reverend LeRoy bit, but not before he featured the famous Ward Singers on his show and the character of Reverend LeRoy joined in with the Gospel songs of the Ward Sisters. The response from the black community across the country was explosive.

His character Geraldine became so popular she began receiving fan mail of her own. Dresses were designed especially for her. She was pampered, she was loved by the world. This character of Geraldine became so big that at one time Flip found it necessary to say, "I will not go into competition with Geraldine."

The first time he hosted "The Tonight Show," Flip picked a routine that could showcase his creative voices. His voices are not imitating anyone, he's not a mimic; his voices are voices he knows, and they come out amusingly because Flip has two things going for him—his innocent appearance and, at the same time, devilish attitude. Remember his recording, "The Devil Made Me Do It"? It was this recording that made Geraldine internationally famous, but it all started out as just a voice.

In his routines he would say, in this falsetto Geraldine voice, "I'm going to see Ray Charles," and the audiences would break up. It was his voice and his antics that created the look for the people. So when the public heard, "The Devil made my buy this dress," the two things had come together, and Geraldine was world famous. Here is a sample:

Flip Wilson Hosting "The Tonight Show"

"Good evening, ladies and gentlemen. I'm glad to be subbing for Johnny Carson, but it seems to cause a

Flip Wilson in a Pensive Mood

FLIP WILSON

little problem. I was in the dressing room when the wardrobe mistress found me there and immediately told me, "This is Johnny Carson's dressing room. What are you doing in Johnny Carson's dressing room? If he catches you in here, it's gonna be the last time you'll be on his show. (Applause)

"We will find a way to overcome some of the obstacles and convince her and everyone at last that NBC is now a fully colored network. This entire week is going to be fun. I'm standing here so cool—I'm not excited. I used to work in a drive-in movie, but it was fun. I used to go around and shine a light in the cars to let people know the movie was over. I got twenty-five dollars a week and all I could see. I'd walk around and say, 'The picture's over, the picture's over.' I tried a lot of things. I came prepared to assume the responsibility of this show. I feel like a weenie roast. I'm the weenie. I operated my own lemonade stand. It was pretty good. It was called 'Flip's Lemonade, All You Can Drink.' But you always got to run into a wise guy. This guy walks up and asks, 'Is this lemonade everything you say it is?' I said, 'You better believe it. It's lemonade like mother used to make.' He said, 'That's got to be some very good lemonade for a dime. You can't beat that.' I said, 'I put extra sugar in it and I pack ice in it.' He said, 'Gimme a glass.' I poured him a glass. He said, 'Gimme another glass.' I said, 'That'll be another dime.' He said, 'The sign says, all you can drink for a dime.' I said, 'You had a glass, didn't you?' He said, 'Yes.' I said, 'Well, that's all you can drink for a dime.'

"People caught on quick, so I decided to try something else. Coming up on the elevator, I heard two guys discussing their golf game. One said to the other, 'How's your golf game going?' The other said, 'Oh, all right.' The first one said, 'I can't believe that.

FLIP WILSON

You and Freddy playing every day, you should be good.' He said, 'Don't mention Freddie's name to me. I don't talk to Freddie. Don't bring his name up anymore, understand?' He said, 'But you and Freddie were such good friends; you guys play golf every other day.' He said, 'Well, not anymore.' 'What happened?' asked the first guy. He said, 'Would you want to play with a guy that cheats, a guy who makes a hole in one gonna take two off? Would you want to play with a guy who steals your clubs while you're watching the ball because somebody already got your bag? You want to play with a guy who runs through the clubhouse and yells, 'Burn, baby, burn'? You want to play with a guy like that?' He said, 'Hell, no!' The other one answered, 'Well, neither do Freddie!' "

The following routines were performed on his "Flip Wilson Show":

Geraldine (with Bing Crosby)

> BING: Happy New Year . . . feeling happy and looking for his Bunny. You got to see it to believe it.
> GERALDINE: Well, you better believe it, you sure ain't gonna get to see it.
> BING: This sure beats anything we got at home. I'm from Cedar Falls.
> GERALDINE: Big Deal! He from Cedar Falls. Is that in America?
> BING: My name's Felix—Mr. Felix Cornwall.
> GERALDINE: Pleased to meet you, Mr. Cornball.
> BING: Cornwall.
> GERALDINE: You wanna bet?
> BING: Are you the waitress?

FLIP WILSON

GERALDINE: We don't use that word around here. Don't come in here with that old "waitress" jive. I'm a "bunny," honey. Bunny Geraldine. This is my first day back. I just got off suspension.

BING: What were you suspended for?

GERALDINE: I forgot to fold the napkins with the clean side out.

BING: I need a drink. Bring me a drink.

GERALDINE: I think I want one, too. I'm tired of posing for the magazine all day.

BING: How 'bout my drink? A little sauce, little toddy for the body.

GERALDINE: Don't rush. You don't get service like this in Cedar Falls. If there is anything you don't like about the service, keep it to yourself. The manager is tired of hearing it. This must be your first time here.

BING: Yes, I'm in town for the convention. I go back home tomorrow.

GERALDINE: We're like ships that pass in the night.

BING: Why don't you come and sit down beside me?

GERALDINE: You devil, you! We're not allowed to sit. That's a Bunny by-law—we can perch, but we can't sit.

BING: What do you mean, perch?

GERALDINE: Just what I said, perch—like this: one foot on the floor at all times. Drink up, honey, I got a quota to get. 'Sides, Johnny Walker wants the bottle back. HE called a few minutes ago and said, "You're holding up the bottle." (Glaring) Look all you want. What you see is a lot more than you gonna get.

BING: How do you call this a drink? It tastes like sarsaparilla!

GERALDINE: Don't touch me. You don't know me. Don't put your hands on me. They got rules against Bunny-touching. Just 'cause I'm dressed like this doesn't mean I'm a loose woman!

BING: I'm sorry. I really am. Will you marry me and be the mother of my children?

GERALDINE: How many you got? You guys are all alike. Every one of you the same. You come in here and say that you want love, but all you want is a shallow friendship.

BING: You know me. I like to be where all the action is. Now what do you recommend for a little fun?

GERALDINE: We're not supposed to recommend.

BING: Well, whisper it in my ear.

GERALDINE: We're not supposed to bend over, either. We don't want to add to the fallout. Those letters on your hat—what do they stand for?

BING: I O P S—International Order of Plumbers.

GERALDINE: How 'bout another drink?

BING: Fine.

GERALDINE: You don't mind if I give you some of mine. I'm not going back over there.

BING: Wait'll I tell them about this back home!

GERALDINE: Watch it!

BING: What's wrong with whirling around?

GERALDINE: You want to whirl, you go home.

BING: What's wrong with a little whirl? One little whirl ain't gonna hurt nobody.

GERALDINE: You must not be aware of Killer.

BING: Who is Killer?

GERALDINE: My boyfriend. I've given him the best years of my life.

BING: I wondered what happened to them.

FLIP WILSON

GERALDINE: The last time a man made a pass at me, it
was a massacre. Killer went crazy! He
started throwing rights, uppercuts.
BING: I could take care of myself.
GERALDINE: But it won't be you he's swinging at!
BING: I'll look out for both of us.
GERALDINE: Yeah, but I can see your epitaph:
Here lies the plumber,
It's the same old song,
Kept puttin' his hands where they
didn't belong.

Flip Wilson and Reverend LeRoy

Reverend LeRoy was the pastor of the Church of the What's
Happening Now. Now, LeRoy was not the kinda guy to tell
you what happened a long time ago, or what's going to
happen in the future. He tells you what's happening . . .
now!

The members of the congregation loved Reverend
LeRoy so much that they got together and chipped in and
built Rev. a new tabernacle. It was really a storefront but
they renovated it and changed the name from Bar-B-Q to
tabernacle. Put a big sign out front—Church of What's
Happening Now: Pastor, Reverend LeRoy.

It was the first day of the service. Early Sunday morning,
down the road, on the path leading through the zoo, comes
Reverend LeRoy.

Now, this Sunday morning, the rain was falling down,
pouring down, and the wind was blowing. In the rain came
Reverend LeRoy. He walked through the zoo.

Standing there, in a cage behind the bars, was a go-rilla.
Yeah, you're laughing, but I realized it was a go-rilla. On
the front of his cage said the name of the animal, said "Go-
rilla." It said, "Be-ware of the Go-rilla"—that's Go-rilla, and
Be-ware. "Be-ware" means, "Watch out for the go-rilla."

FLIP WILSON

As Rev. approaches the cage, he sees the go-rilla. Rev. thinks it's a man in jail who's had his civil rights violated.

Rev. stops in front of the cage, and he says, "Say, brother, say, brother, why? Why have they got you behind those bars? Whatever they said you did, you didn't do it. I know an innocent face when I see one—but you didn't do it, brother.

"Just look at the hairs hanging down in your nasty face!" he said. "Brother, they won't even let you wash your nasty face. Look, they even got you drinking out of a trough! A man got to get pretty low to drink from a trough!

"We're going to do something about this. I'm going right down to the tabernacle and get the members to draw up a petition and send it to Washington. We're going to do something, brother!

"All I got is a raincoat and a pack of chewing gum, but you can have them. I'm gonna give them to you."

He walked over and dropped the raincoat and extended his hand, which the go-rilla clasped gently.

Rev. said, "Oh, brother, I'm going to see you in a little while." He went to pull back, and he felt the go-rilla tighten up. The pain shot up his arm and down his back.

He said, "Brother, I told you I would see you in a little while."

Then Rev. heard his spine . . . snap.

Rev. said, "Brother, I will see you in a little while."

He snapped against the cage. He twisted his shoulders through the bars and broke both shoulders getting them in there.

"Brother, wait a minute!"

The go-rilla snapped his neck; he had a handful of the man's neck. A handful of neck doesn't leave too much neck! Has anyone had a handful of your neck?

The go-rilla picked him up and walked to both sides of the cage, swung him around, dropped him, then stomped on him, then picked him up and swung him out between the bars.

Flip Wilson with Redd Foxx

Rev. got up, brushed off his clothes, and walked over to the cage. He said, "Brother, I'm talking to you."

The go-rilla laid back, and Rev. continued, "You're not a man. You act like a go-rilla, that's the way you act. And whatever they said you did, you did. You did it, yes, you did it. I'm in a position to send a petition to Washington all right, to see that you get the electric chair. And, oh, yes, about that shaggy hair hanging down your nasty face—I hope they keep you in there so long, it will cover your shaggy carcass!"

RICHARD PRYOR

RICHARD PRYOR

<u>That Nigger Is Crazy</u> . . . is the title of Richard Pryor's album, and it says it all. He's a mind-blower—possibly the funniest man on the scene today.

He's an actor, a comic, and onstage he's outrageous. His subject matter is always offbeat. His interpretation of birth is a classic. His portrayals are always very poignant. He's always right on target. There's no mistaking his characterizations; it's the "Nigger." No one does him with such accuracy.

When he comes onstage, his opening line is: "Thanks for coming. I hope I'm funny, 'cause niggers kick ass after they have spent their money and you ain't funny." He follows this with that funny little laugh that's so contagious. Standing there, he looks so innocent: he's long and lean, almost cadaverous in certain poses with his long, thin arms protruding awkwardly from his jacket. His fingers are also long and tapered and he uses them to great advantage as he expresses himself.

His performances are made up of different variations on the same theme—the nigger. It's the poolroom nigger, the barbershop nigger, the hustler nigger—and he's brilliant. To some who are thin-skinned, they say he uses those terms strictly for shock value. Some people get offended because he seems to make the cat in the street his main character. There's no doubt he knows his subject matter very well because he definitely relates to everybody. His audiences are made up of as many whites as blacks. Of course, black people flock to see him because he's talking to and about them.

His most famous bit is called "The Wino." In this piece, Richard plays all the parts, and watching it you can see each character clearly. Even on the record, you can get the picture. Often he'll remind you of Chaplin. He is a brilliant pantomimist.

His dialogue is sprinkled generously with four-letter words and his phrases have the audience rolling. For example, he'll be talking about the guys in the barbershop,

RICHARD PRYOR

saying how they'd bet on anything. Here you can see his expressions change, and you can visualize the two characters speaking: "Betcha. . . . Betcha. . . . Betcha a hunert." "Man, you ain't got a hunert!" One says to the other, "Yeah, that's a hunert," and the other comes back with, "I ain't gotta show you shit!" It's a piece that almost everyone can relate to—the big-mouth who knows it all and then cops out.

He talks about the white man in his portrayal of the westerner visiting the whorehouse: "You're always coming over here looking for black girls. Why don't you bring some of your white bitches over here?" The white dude answers, "Now it ain't no need to talk dirty."

No one is spared with Richard Pryor. Even the Vietnamese. He calls them America's new niggers. He says in his album, after those families rushed and adopted those poor babies from Vietnam, "Hey, if you want to adopt something foreign, there's some black babies that need adopting. Wait until after a few years of looking at the slanty eyes, you gonna hear them say, 'Ain't your eyes never gonna round off?'"

Or his encounter with Big-Ass Bertha in the whorehouse (here he sticks out his behind and assumes a pose of Big Bertha). She says she wants twenty dollars for her trick, and Richard comes back with, "Twenty dollars for some pussy? Bitch, for twenty dollars your pussy will have to call me by my name!"

When he meets up with Count Blackula, he says, "Count Blackula, what kinda name is that for a nigger? You dig blood, huh, why don't you go to the blood bank? It's just down the street. I hope your ass gets sickle cell!"

Once, when Marlon Brando came in to see his performance and he introduced Brando from the stage (as a rule he'd never do it, but even Richard respected Brando), Richard said, "What could I say about this dude, except he's an acting motherfucker!" Brando cracked up.

There was a time that David Janssen came in to see

RICHARD PRYOR

Richard, and again, when he introduced him he added his accolade, "You're a running motherfucker!" referring to Janssen's old television series "The Fugitive."

Since making the movie Lady Sings the Blues, Richard's career has been going more and more toward films. His fantastic performance in that film proved beyond a doubt that he is a personality to be reckoned with.

To say that he uses four-letter words solely for shock value is to overlook the brilliance of the man. At times, when he runs into hecklers, he has one response that stops them. He simply says, "Fuck you." It stops them cold. There is no doubt about it, Richard is the leader of the "Fuck it" Society.

Once, when Johnny Carson invited him on his "Tonight Show," the subject of nicknames came up. Carson asked Richard, "As a youngster, what nickname did they call you?" Richard answered, "Skinny nigger." Carson turned red while Richard sat there looking innocent. The audience roared, mostly at his guts.

A lot of people get mad because Richard uses the word nigger throughout his dialogue. Many think it's unnecessary. But you only have to walk down any street that's black and you'll hear what Richard says on any corner. So, for interpretation, he's right on target.

Some of Richard's very deep feelings sometimes come out in his routines. In his routine on birth, he starts off by explaining, "The stork didn't bring me. My mother and father laid down and fucked . . . and my mother brought me out . . . or pushed me out." Then he goes into the pantomime of being born. It's a very sensitive performance, accurate and, as usual, brilliant. By the time he finally gets to the baby's cry, the audience is almost devastated. It's the accuracy of it that makes it acceptable. It's truth.

At no time do you hear Richard tell a joke. His works and monologues are conversation pieces. His confrontation with the police, his tenure in jail, all come out as funny

RICHARD PRYOR

bits and pieces: "I went to jail to find justice, and that's what I found, just us," meaning all of the inmates were black.

Richard proved himself to be totally unique at the very beginning of his career when he did such wonderful bits as the weight lifter in school and the fairy-tale classic "Rumplestiltskin." It was only after he was a big hit that he changed. His language became a big factor, and he began to use phrases the way they were supposed to be said. He began to interpret the winos, pimps, and whores—that part of our society that was scorned. Richard was the first to bring these characters to the stage in the form of hilarious pieces that tore into our consciousness to rip all the covers off.

His encounters with the law, his having relations with white women, his snorting coke—all of these became his subject matter. There was nothing too sacred for his repertoire. His mind was preoccupied with one thing—truth. After ten years in nightclubs, television, and a string of films that were rated mediocre (whose best features were often his brief appearance in them), Richard finally proved to the world that he was a great talent.

Richard Pryor was born in Peoria, Illinois. He grew up in an all-black neighborhood but went to an integrated school. "When I was a little boy," he said, "I was in love with this white girl in my class. I once brought her a scratchboard as a gift—one of those gray cardboard things you draw on, then you lift it up and the picture's gone. The next day her father came to school and said to me, 'Don't you dare give my daughter a present!' When I told my father about it, he just shook his head. You see, nobody had told me about racism, but he knew.

"One of my most traumatic experiences was when I went to see a Little Beaver movie. When it was over, I tried to get back behind the screen. I thought Little Beaver would be there. I wanted to talk to him. I never thought to myself that Little Beaver was white. I never thought in

Richard Pryor

color, just feelings. My heroes at the time were the same as all kids. I wanted to be like John Wayne."

Color now is a factor in all of his interpretations: "Black people can't dissasociate themselves from issues of race because we're living in a white world. The time for being white is over. I have no use for anyone who never lets you forget what color they are. My grandmother always told me, 'Son, one thing a white man can't take from you is the knowledge. You take some 63-year-old cat on the street, ugly, spit coming out of his mouth, he's still got something you can't have. You can't say he didn't see that gutter or he didn't drink the wine. That's the knowledge.'

"I love what I do very much. It's the only thing in my life that never hurt me, that's given me fulfillment and let me have dignity—never belittled me. I'll be all right as long as there is show business and people will laugh. If they change that around and people don't laugh, if they stopped laughing, I wouldn't want to live."

COMEDIANS OF THE SEVENTIES

THE SEVENTIES

Many comedians on the horizon now come from writing stables across the country—à la Woody Allen and Dick Cavett, who wrote for Johnny Carson and Jack Paar, and later turned performers.

PAUL MOONEY

Billed as the Black Tornado, Paul Mooney followed this same formula. He began as a writer and one of his most famous clients is Richard Pryor. Mooney originated the line that Pryor used as the title of his album <u>That Nigger Is Crazy</u>.

Mooney, who did the casting on the first "Richard Pryor TV Special," now is performing his own material—or hearing his own lines being read to him years later.

But he also faces much resistance. Not only is his satire biting, but many accuse him of copying Pryor. In defense of his style, Mooney says, "I'm into my own thing. I don't in any way come over like Richard. Don't get me wrong, I love Richard. And, of course, he was a first for us. So naturally, anyone with offbeat material is immediately accused of doing Richard.

"I guess it's natural for people to compare me to Richard. I say, well, I can't be in better company. Even putting me in the same class as Richard, to me that's a compliment. But I do try to be me. It's just that some people get uptight because I don't tap dance. But I can hambone!" And then he goes into the routine he does on hambone, and you always wind up laughing at him doing it.

JIMMIE "J.J." WALKER

Jimmie Walker became an overnight success playing the role of a teenager on the hit television series "Good Times." The series, which stars Esther Rolle, also features

THE SEVENTIES

a group of accomplished actors and actresses, but it's the role of J.J. that comes off the funniest.

"I started out doing comedy with a group that was on the militant black thing," he says. "I was like their opening act. The group's name was The Poets. At that time I was the hit of the campus; I was doing shows for the student body.

"At the time, I used to see a lot of Bill Cosby, who was my idol. Even Richard Pryor was one of my heroes back then. Someone suggested that I go to the Improv, a local hangout on 44th Street, where comedians came around and worked out their material for television.

"In those days, comics like Stiller and Meara, Gabe Kaplan, Rodney Dangerfield, everybody was working on their 'Ed Sullivan Show' routine. I'd overhear people like Gabe come in and say, 'I've got to work out my new routine I'm doing on "The Merv Griffin Show."' I would stand around and be impressed.

"In those days we had to hang around to get on the stage. Most of the time it would be around three o'clock before new guys like me would get to perform. It was Bette Midler that first told Bud Freeman (the club's owner) about me. He wasn't too impressed because, after all, he had all the top comics coming into his place, working out their new material. He couldn't care less about cats like me and Freddie Prinze. We were the newcomers, so we had to wait. I guess that's why most of us had to start out with stuff about the audience. We couldn't rely on material. I don't care what kind of material you have, at three o'clock in the morning nobody wants to hear it. So we would try to get some rapport with the audience.

"Well, I went on a couple of times and didn't do too bad, and from that I started doing commercials. I had about seven when they were casting for the show 'Good Times.' I had done a 'Rowan and Martin Television Special' and Pat Kirkland asked for one of my tapes. She wanted to show it to Norman Lear. I wasn't putting too much faith in it, so that's the way I gave it to her.

THE SEVENTIES

"I went on tour doing about sixty colleges. In 1973 Jack Paar made a brief return to television, and I was booked on the show. I remember I was nervous, one of the few times I was ever really nervous. Jack Paar said to me, 'Don't worry about it. I started Dick Gregory, Godfrey Cambridge, and you're going to be all right.' And it was. I got some good results from that show.

"I finally got myself a good manager, Jerry Kuscnich. It was while I was doing the warmups for 'Calucci's Department,' which starred Jimmy Coco, that I got the word that I had gotten the role of J.J. It was something unexpected. I guess that's why I got it.

"But it allowed me the chance to have a lot of fun in the role. I found out I could adjust to television without too many problems. I think what happens to actors is they're always looking for some kind of motivation in every word, and they become very uptight. I don't have those hangups. I try to get as much fun out of it as I can. I'd rather take a chance and use some creativity with some scenes. I've gotten into trouble a few times, but I think it's necessary to take chances and find out that your suggestions sometimes work. I guess that's why each season is fun to me.

"I like playing J.J. He's someone I can relate to. Remember, I was a teenager in a Harlem ghetto. I'm a product of that generation that felt that we could do anything if we wanted to. I could talk my ghetto talk to white people and they found they were in the same boat as me.

"I don't dig the thing 'star.' I love being a performer. I work hard at my craft. That's why when we're shooting in L.A., I work out at The Comedy Store. It helps me in what I do as an entertainer—comedy. And the only way you can keep your timing at its peak is to continually hone up on your routines. And the only way to do that is to work at it. And I do.

"I've got a group of writers and we work on projects together. I want to do all kinds of comedy—series, plays, and material for recordings. I think it's the least that the

THE SEVENTIES

Black Prince can do to spread happiness throughout the world. But as for being a star, it's all right, but I love television. I say it's Dy-No-Mite!"

FRANKLYN AJAYE

Franklyn Ajaye began his career with a recording contract. He wasn't in show business long before he had a big sign up at A&M Records with his name on it. One of his more recent A&M albums is called Don't Smoke Dope, Fry Your Hair.

It was while he was in college that he began to take seriously the thought of becoming a comedian. As he tells it, "I took a class up at the Lee Strasburg Institute last year. I think that was the turning point for me because it was a twelve-week course on film acting. What it did for me was to expose me to discussion of techniques, but it was a very intellectual approach to acting. I took some notes. I enjoyed the class because, number one, it freed me. I think I've become a better comedian in the last year.

"Because of that class, I stopped standing at the mike. I take the mike in hand now and walk around the stage. It freed me physically. But as far as acting is concerned, I felt my own way around the filming of Sweet Revenge and Car Wash. A lot of people think that comedians are not good actors. I don't know why. Look at Bill Cosby. Go back to Sid Caesar. I feel that comedy and acting are really related. I don't know why they think that comedians can't act.

"I was reading an article by Robert Kline in the magazine Genesis. They asked him something that made a lot of sense to me. It put things in their right perspective about people having an image of a comedian. When the comedian talks seriously and it comes off serious, it's a contradiction of what the public has seen and it seems that much more dramatic.

THE SEVENTIES

"I feel comfortable doing my own standup comedy, but, to put it bluntly, I don't like comedic acting. It's too hard. There's no spontaneity. It's a burden. Like Richard Pryor. He's under a hell of a burden. When they put him into a movie, it's got to be funny. He has to take someone else's words and someone else's situation that might not be that funny and make something out of it. Someone else has written something that they think is funny, yet you might not think it's a damn bit funny. But if you don't play it funny enough to please them, they might come down hard on you.

"Dramatic acting is different. Doing Sweet Revenge was pretty nice. They helped me a lot in that, especially Stockard Channing, the picture's star. I felt intimidated by the fact that they were all professionals. I knew the director had faith in me and I wanted to justify that faith. How many directors are going to take that kind of a chance with a new person? They won't. Not on a major film. He could have gone with an established actor, but he saw something in me that I didn't know I had.

"There are two or three different types of actors in that film. One guy, who played Andy, had a very disciplined approach. I thought he was good. He worked on his lines every night. I looked at him and thought maybe I should be doing the same thing. Stockard knew the character she was playing, and she would come to the set with an idea of how her lines were to be played. She had a looser approach and that helped me. If I wasn't prepared for a particular day, I wouldn't worry about it.

"It was watching Richard Pryor that gave me the courage to be me onstage. I couldn't relate to Bob Hope and Alan King. But it was when I saw Richard that I said to myself, 'Wow, I dig where the cat's coming from!' I could relate.

"I often wondered who wanted to hear about my background. After Richard, I had a point of reference. I saw Richard do black characters I knew and came up with some

THE SEVENTIES

from my own background, and I knew in what direction I would go.

"After I got out of college, I came to the realization that I didn't want no nine-to-five gig. I hated authority and I knew some dude who had the power to hire and fire over me would get me mad and I'd say a quick 'Fuck it' and walk out. I also know that there are a lot of hassles over you in show business—a lot of people who really control your life. But I sat down one day and said to myself, 'Hey, I'm funny, and I'm talented. I can make people laugh. Okay, this is what I can do well and I don't mind working at it, because when you dig something, it don't seem like work. I think when you make people laugh, people like you for it. It gives people a good feeling to be around someone who can make them laugh. I think people want people around when they're funny."

THE
BLACK WOMAN
IN COMEDY

THE LADIES

Women, in general, are not well represented in comedy. This is even more true in the case of black women. Their numbers are almost nil, and one is forced to wonder why this is so.

The truth of the matter is that black women do go into comedy—and probably in the same proportionate numbers as whites. The problem is that the black woman is limited because she never got over the black fat-mammy syndrome, the Aunt Jemima. Therefore, there's no way she can get the Lucille Ball or Carol Burnett-type roles.

On the screen, there suddenly was an abundance of the Hattie McDaniel-type black women whose sole function was to play the servants. For instance, there was Lillian Randolph, who played the role of Birdie, a good old acid-talking housekeeper, with Danny Thomas. Even Pearl Bailey once played Bob Hope's housekeeper. And, of course, there was Ethel Waters, who played "Beulah" on television.

The list of those whose talents were smothered in a housedress or an apron (or both) is long. The easiest way for the black female performer to escape playing these inane parts was by going the singing route. It was far better to become a singing star, playing the big clubs and getting hit records, than to be subjected to the type of comedic acting that was required of an Aunt Jemima-type. No doubt we lost out on many great performers who might have gone on to become comedy stars were it not for the music business.

In the days of the variety shows, there were many black women who tried to get into the business as comediennes. But with the emergence of the single performer, not many black women ever made it alone.

JACKIE "MOMS" MABLEY

The only black woman who lasted, even through the era of television, was the funny and wonderful late Jackie

THE LADIES

"Moms" Mabley. Moms, as she was called and wanted to be called, was always loved by everyone. She was well known in the black community long before white audiences became familiar with her. She played the black circuits all through the South and was always on the best bills that played the Apollo Theatre. For years she was a headliner at the Howard in Washington, D.C., and the Royal Theatre in Baltimore.

It was very late in her life when television found her. She became a favorite guest on such programs as the Mike Douglas and Merv Griffin shows.

Moms was a very close friend of Redd Foxx and Slappy White, and this trio was considered the Big Three of black comedy for a long time. She naturally acted like their mom, always advising them on both personal and career matters. Additionally, Slappy costarred with her in the one and only movie that was written and designed especially for her talents, Amazing Grace.

She was determined that she was going to finish the picture, and she did. But it was shortly after that we said goodbye to Moms. She laid the groundwork for others to follow. She was a talented and funny woman whose strong suit was playing the homespun type. Her toothless grin, the funny shoes that appeared to be on the wrong feet, and her starched housedress with a little of the petticoat always showing created instant hysterics—especially when she would utter her famous opening line, "But I'm clean!"

Moms had a deep love for the late John F. Kennedy. On his death, she wrote and sang a song that was dedicated to him. She later recorded "Martin, Bobby and John," which she sang with such feeling that she made tears come to your eyes.

Moms always had a love affair going with a star, too. During her vaudeville days, she was in love with Cab Calloway. She would always sing the blues about the way Cab treated her: "He treats me so bad, chillun; he's a mistreatin' dog. He runs around wid all the chorus girls and cheat on me! Who needs him? Me!"

THE LADIES

Her recordings are still sold in record stores throughout the land. This great artist's work will be around for many years to come, and her style can be studied by other female hopefuls. Moms Mabley was the last of a breed. Women who distort their appearance for laughs no longer exist. Costume comedy has been discarded by women. On the other hand, television has brought us some new female stars who are comedy actresses.

ISABEL SANFORD

In this new group, there is Isabel Sanford, who stars in the CBS-TV series "The Jeffersons." Isabel is the typical actress of today who can read funny lines, as opposed to standing in front of an audience and saying funny things off the top of her head or from a designed monologue. Although the style for television is not easy, and it does call for good acting ability, Isabel Sanford is one of the best. Her repartee is right on target for television, and her talents are a major factor in the success of her series.

ESTHER ROLLE

Another comedienne who is emerging from TV is Esther Rolle, who stars each week on the television series "Good Times," which introduced Jimmie "J.J." Walker. Esther was a straight dramatic actress from the Broadway stage who one day found herself playing Florida, the maid, on the TV sitcom "Maude." (It was from the spinoff of Esther's Florida characterization that "Good Times" was born.) She had to convert to a wisecracking maid with a bent for one-upmanship on a liberal, white female who herself was striving for liberation. While she had a black maid on whom she could try out all her good deeds, Maude had a hard time handling her own plight as a liberal thinking, liber-

THE LADIES

ated white woman. The spinoff gave Florida a chance to have a family and give the world a glimpse at black America, living in a Chicago ghetto. Esther Rolle is an accomplished actress, whether her role be comedic or dramatic; there's never any doubt that she can handle it.

JA'NET DUBOIS

From the same series, "Good Times," came the funny role of the goodhearted but wacky neighbor Winona, played by Ja'net DuBois. Ja'net is one of our finer actresses. She can play everything from stark drama to broad comedy. Television fortunately has captured some of her zaniness, but there is much more depth to Ja'net. However, like most female artists, roles are hard to come by and when a black actress gets a chance at a series, she's not going to be too picky about playing slapstick. It shows the versatility of some of our actresses who, because of their sheer talent, brought their characters life and then sustained them.

COSTARS

Other female comedy actresses include Theresa Merritt, who costarred with Clifton Davis on the now-defunct television series "That's My Mama." A newcomer to this set is little Shirly Hemphill, a standup comedienne who is making the adjustment to TV with no difficulty. She's at The Comedy Store in Hollywood, one of the few places that really turns out comedians. The Comedy Store is where aspiring young comedians can get their chance to work out routines and try them before live audiences. Here, a novice without any credentials can walk up onstage and begin, if she or he has the guts. Shirley Hemphill had the guts and the material. She's fast and sharp and says many bright things. She's one of the young breed that uses the

language as it is and is spoken from the background of the new people today. Her popularity comes from television, so this new exposure will no doubt change much of her presentation in the future.

La Wanda Page of "Sanford and Son," playing the role of Aunt Esther, has come over the tube as a real character. Her wisecracks and her biting tongue in response to Fred Sanford's insults are one of the high points of that series.

There are a number of wonderful comediennes, but, of course, the field is dominated by men. It's a very chauvinistic profession. The big laughs about women were when the male comedian would always lambast his wife's cooking, her mother, her spending his hard-earned money or wrecking his car. These are all the subjects that have ruled the comedy world for years.

But, like everything else, the thinking of the world has changed. Women stopped letting themselves be the butt of men's jokes. Women began to answer back by asking for equal time. But the strange thing that happened was that when they did it, they were considered aggressive, unfeminine, unladylike, and bitchy.

Also, it's hard for an audience to accept a woman who uses four-letter words. It doesn't fit her image, they argue, but the very image they're talking about is the image that men have of women; it has nothing to do with the woman herself.

Shirley Hemphill says that a lot of men feel intimidated and inhibited, because she's so outgoing and honest. They feel uncomfortable and say she's unfeminine. So perhaps women have simply been conditioned to think that if they put themselves up to ridicule, it isn't ladylike.

Most men don't like comediennes because they say that comediennes talk too much, especially about their secrets. They're all shook up when they realize that a broad has peeped their whole card.

Some of the finest comediennes are white—Phyllis Diller, Joan Rivers, Totie Fields, to name just a few. These

THE LADIES

women are brilliant, and not a black woman among them. Isn't that strange? Not really, when you analyze it correctly. For one thing, dignity has been a long time coming for black women. It took a lifetime for black women to obtain it and now that they have a chance at last, they're not about to throw it away on laughter.

Now that women of all colors are coming out from under their yokes, they are beginning to laugh about it, the same as any other deprived group. Some of our most prestigious women in the world could bring a laugh, like Barbara Jordan, who looks like Aunt Jemima and talks like Bobby Kennedy. Then, there is Shirley Chisholm, the presidential candidate. Her campaign was a joke. And to add insult to injury, even the all-male black caucus ostracized her. Talk about your brothers!

A black woman's biggest problem has been her man. She sang about him; she sang the blues. She wallowed in the mire of self-pity; her man is gone—woe is me! But today's black women would say: "That nigger is gone. Good. He ain't no good, no how. Has two tits that don't milk, a belly button that don't button, two balls that don't bounce, and an ass that don't work. Nigger . . . you need a job!"

Today's black woman is finally liberated. Now, at long last—after all her life, through the sweat of her brow, pulling her man through—she can finally go out and work for herself!

There is a commercial that shows a black woman on her knees, scrubbing floors, and a voice saying, "My mother scrubbed floors so I could get an education." They've got to be kidding! Today's woman would take that same mop and hit her man right across the chops and say, "Nigger, you need a job!"

There's another commercial that shows an embarrassed housewife when the kids bring her a soiled shirt and sing, "Ring around the collar," implying that it's her fault, that she didn't wash it clean enough. Today's woman would say, "Tell that nigger to wash his neck!"

THE LADIES

NORMA MILLER

Me, I'm Norma Miller and I'm a comedienne. I became a comedienne at the insistence of my friends (and coauthor of this book, Redd Foxx). Redd would always tell me, "Norma, we don't have any black women represented in comedy. You're not going to be able to dance all your life, so you better start thinking about talking. You could last a whole lot longer talking than you could ever do dancing."

So, with this logic and with my earning power as a dancer dwindling down to zero, I tackled the world of comedy. I found out one thing very quickly. Being funny is serious. I was funny until I tried to be. And like I always said when I started down this road, "If I knew then what I know now, you might not have had this one."

It was ten years later when I took the next plunge. I completely abandoned dance and began a career totally in comedy. I served my entire ten-year apprenticeship under Redd Foxx, which began in 1967 at his Los Angeles club. I began to work for him as his hostess and his ticket-taker at the door.

The years have been slipping faster than I'd like to think, and I realize I'm not twenty-one anymore. I'm not thirty-one anymore—and I can go on like this for years and years and years.

It's not a put-down type of comedy anymore. Telling the truth is what makes a routine believable. Take me, for instance. I'm now, after all these years, a spinster. There was a time when I was considered to be a broad who said no once too often. But that's not the case anymore. Whenever I'm asked by a gentleman why I've never gotten married, I simply turn to him and say, "Because none of you bastards ever asked me!"

Of course, they asked me everything else. But when you're young and you don't know what's happening, when you hear questions, you just don't know the answers. Now

**Top: Moms Mabley Surrounded by her Loyal Friends; bottom:
Norma Miller and Her Dancers**

that I'm grown and I've got all the answers, nobody is asking me anything. After believing all these years that early to bed and early to rise would make a gal healthy, wealthy, and wise, all I ended up was healthy, sexless, and single! And I've been single so long, I'm a senior single.

A spinster—lots of people call me an old maid. I am not. I am a spinster. To some there is no difference, but there is a difference—and <u>vive la différence</u>! Admitting to the world that you're an old maid is like telling the world you've grown old on the vine and you ain't been plucked. I've not only been plucked, I've been boiled in oil and fooled and screwed by the fickle finger of fate—and ain't even been called "Baby."

Women of this world have got to start to get it together, because the men have. Of course, they call it Gay Lib. As fast as women's lib is putting the men out of their beds, the Gay Lib is taking them in!

Take it from me, Bill Bailey never is coming home. Last time I saw him, he was strolling down Hollywood Boulevard holding hands with his new interest. I said, "There they go—Romeo and Romeo!"

The strange thing about a relationship between a man and a woman is that just when you think you can lay back and begin to enjoy that togetherness, when you don't have to worry about the Pill, that's when those bastards throw you over for another chick—and a younger one, too!

Today when you're in the beauty shop getting your hair done, who's sitting next to you getting theirs done? He is. Do you realize that today more men are getting transplants than women? Men today are getting more facelifts than women, but what they <u>should</u> have lifted, they <u>don't</u>!

Today <u>he</u> is the sex object. The competition out here today is very keen; women are outnumbering men almost five to one, and what's left we've got to share with? Homosexuals, bisexuals, transexuals—and I'm a heterosexual. There's nothing worse than being heterosexual and having nobody to heterosex with!

THE LADIES

Today they tell you to do your own thing. They've got to be kidding. Sometimes to do your own thing, you need a friend. Remember, sometimes it takes two to tango. I know with the liberation of women, women are now seeking equality in the bedroom. I don't need equality in the bedroom at this stage of life. I need a bed warmer. I'm just plain fed up with going to bed with . . . arthritis. I'd love to cuddle up with something nice and cuddly, but what I'd like and what I get are two different things entirely.

For a gal who digs men the most, what I get looks like something I dig up. That last date was a beaut. He looked like Idi Amin's twin—big, black, and burly. His hair looked like he swallowed a hand grenade. And stoned out of his head. He was so high he fell up. He was the last of the big-time spenders. He had a charge account at McDonald's.

There was a time that a woman without a man was like a fish out of water. Today Gloria Steinem says a woman without a man is like a fish without a bicycle. Women today are coming out of the closet. They're getting involved. They're not laying there and taking it no more.

Once it was Mr. Smith that went to Washington; now it's Mrs. Smith that's going to Washington. And she's having a ball, screwing them all, and telling it all. The women are taking over because only through women will there be peace. Men want power. Women want peace. Every woman in the world knows the meaning of a good peace. With that, I leave you, as I'm going where I can find a good peace.

REDD FOXX

REDD FOXX

Redd Foxx tells his story in his own words:

When I first started out in the business, the blackface comedian was something I resented strongly. I used to see this in St. Louis and Chicago where I grew up and couldn't figure out why a man being black had to black up his face. I just couldn't see no reason for it.

Even the dialect I resented. When Slappy White and I first began to work together back in 1948, the first thing I did was to take the de's and dem's and doe's out of his mouth. We were not going to talk like that. I knew I didn't need no dialect to be funny, so I never used it.

A nigger don't need no makeup to be funny, anyway. Funny is in the word—the mouth—not the clothes or what he wears.

But it wasn't till I got the reputation for being a "blue" comedian that I began to be noticed. I used to do routines about the black neighborhoods where I grew up. Out of this, I developed a routine I called "Racetrack," where I would go into a fast-paced takeoff on a racetrack announcer. I used to color it up by naming the horses "Motherfucker" and "Shitkicker" and so on, and pretty soon people started requesting it in the clubs.

Another one of my earlier routines that went over big was the soap commercial I'd do like a radio announcer. I called that one "Fugg and Sugg."

Then there was my bit on Tarzan, which was probably the most popular of all. I told the true story about how Tarzan got his yell:

"As Tarzan was swinging in the trees, he notices that Jane is in trouble; an alligator has spotted her and starts to go after her. Tarzan hears her scream and swings over to her on a vine. Then he yells to Jane, "Jane, grab vine, grab vine!" Jane reaches up and grabs without looking at what she's grabbing. She just grabs . . . and Tarzan yells . . . "Ooooh . . . ahhhh . . . oooooh!"

REDD FOXX

I did all these routines on my early records for Dootsie Williams on the Dooto Records label. They must have gone over on wax, too, because they sold better than anyone ever thought they would, including me.

The comedian, the comic, the humorist, the clown—these are the different styles of comedians, and you've got to find out what fits your own personality best if you're thinking about becoming one of them.

But everybody ain't born funny. Some people practice and they can do some funny routines and get good at it. Some cats got a funny look, a funny face. They're the lucky ones. But some cats don't find out they're not right for the business until they've wasted a lot of time and effort over it.

One of the dudes that influenced me when I first came along was Sandy Burns. He was a blackface, but he was funny with that long head of his that he would turn sideways and always give that funny look. Sandy was just a natural.

But that Lenny Bruce was the greatest human being I ever met. He was honest. He said things that were not conventional to say. But they needed being said and Lenny was the first to say them. He was crucified for telling the truth. He was a great influence on me.

I remember when I'd go on stage to do a show, whether it was television or stage, and some bastard would have the nerve to tell me what I could not say. He's going to assume that I'm going to say something offcolor, to his way of thinking, just because he hears that I say things that are not considered "in the best of taste." He's not giving me credit for having any kind of intelligence. He's just going to assume things. I say fuck 'em! Who needs it?

The argument whether something is obscene or not should be left up to the individual to decide. Why should you tell me that what I say is wrong? If you don't want to hear it, split. Don't try to tell others that what I say should

not be heard. That's the same bullshit that destroyed Lenny Bruce. Dirty is in the mind of the beholder, not in the word itself.

In today's society we're seeing a change in the thinking of the paying public. The people are telling the government that it's full of shit. It says one thing to the people and it acts differently when it comes down to their own moral standards. It's like the dude that's passing the laws against the chicks—prostitutes, as they say in the courts; and it's the same dude doing the prosecuting that you see going into the whorehouse. (Today they call them massage parlors.)

Dirty language is supposed to be liked by blacks. Black humor is basically dirty because today everybody wants to get down to the nitty-gritty of things. We're telling it like it is. The language of today is supposed to be black-oriented. I say bullshit!

Today the average person is not shocked when he hears the word <u>fuck</u>. It's used by the average person. More Americans use the word than ever before. The statement, "Who gives a fuck?" is as American as you can get. It's not black or white nor brown nor red; it's as much a part of the American language as <u>ain't</u> is.

Now, when young comics come to me for advice, I tell them to stay away from material that would keep them off the airways. I also tell them to work anywhere, anytime. There still ain't no substitute for experience. You've got to learn your craft, and comedy takes craftsmanship. The more you work at it, the better you will be at it.

At times, young comedians start out by trying to steal someone else's material. I tell them that's a mistake. It takes a long time to develop a style that you can call your own, and if you're using someone else's stuff, you'll wind up being second best—and that's like an also-ran horse.

I tell these young cats to try to keep their material fresh by adding something to it every time they work. This way

REDD FOXX

their stuff never comes off stale. The best advice I could give is to tell them to try to write a joke every day. That's seven jokes a week, thirty a month. At the end of a year, you'll have enough material to get yourself a job, I tell them. And leave mine alone!

A typical example of how a comic can spring his own trap by stealing was this cat who got away with doing my material for years. And he became very good at it, too. Everything was cool as long as he worked the small clubs he'd been working in. Nobody ever questioned his interpretation.

But one day he was booked at the Tropicana in Las Vegas. This was a giant step for this cat, his first shot at the big time. So, he got there, and he walked out on the stage and the curtain was closed behind him. And his opening line was:

"How do you like that? The first time I get to work with a white band, they close the curtain on me!" Ordinarily it would have been a funny opener, but there was no doubt about it, it was done in my style. And so was the rest of the act.

The buyer, catching him at the Trop, was said to have remarked, "He's funny, but why should I pay for a third-rate Redd Foxx, when I can get the real thing at the Hilton?" The comic's show was canceled immediately.

It was a good lesson for this cat. You can't work at what someone else has created and still be successful. Besides, who'd want to rip me off, anyway? I work basic. All I do is talk about what you do. If you don't do it, I don't talk about it.

Like the story I tell about my old St. Bernard, Crotch. Crotch was a big fellow and I loved that animal. So I tell it this way:

"I'm over fifty and I'm too old to use the term doodoo. Besides, you can't feed a 190-pound St. Bernard ten cans of Alpo and expect him to doodoo. He shits, and I have a whole backyard to prove it!"

REDD FOXX

I know, some of you folks out there don't like hearing them kind of words—or even just reading them—but I want you to know that all I'm trying to do is bring a little laughter into your life—and if I've offended anyone by my straightforwardness, dear reader, frankly—I don't give a shit!

But seriously, folks, I just want you to know that for years I was operating under a terrible misconception. Because I am a black man, I thought it would be in very bad taste to offend anyone with vulgarity. So, I didn't. I watched my language and stuff because they used to tell me it would keep me out of the big clubs. Well, I didn't play the big clubs anyway, so after a while, I figured screw that! I went back to being blue-black.

Which reminds me of a recent television show, when Dean Martin roasted me. One of the comedians on the panel, I forget who, said, "Redd Foxx is a real American—as American as apple pie. His name is Redd, his hair is white, and his material is blue!"

I always say, "Fuck convention." My bag has always been to talk about things like sex and everything that most people don't discuss in public.

Take snot, for instance. Everybody's got some snot in their nose, but no one talks about it! Or when I say, "Fuck Kate Smith!" I say that in my act and make the audience join in. But what I'm doing there is defying something sacred. Everybody loves Kate Smith, even me. But I say it anyway and the folks out in the audience just eat it up.

It's like patriotism. I'm as patriotic as anyone and I love America, too, but I ain't gonna suck the flag! (That's another line I use that always works.)

To me, comedy is a series of things that have happened in your life. With me, it's always the saddest things that make you laugh the loudest.

Like when I was growing up as a small boy in St. Louis. We was poooor! So once a week, I think it was Wednes-

REDD FOXX

days, my grandfather would come upstairs to Grandma to tell her that the garbageman had come. And Grandma would yell down to Grandpa, "Well, tell him to leave three cans!"

And when the civil rights marchers was parading through Selma and getting it from the white-sheet wearers, I used to say, "I ain't gonna do no marching nonviolently. Ain't no way I'm gonna let a cracker go upside my head with a stick and I do nothin' but hum 'We Shall Overcome.' I'm going to cut him. I'm from St. Louis, and we wake up buck-naked with our knife on. But I don't want to overcome. I'd go crazy!"

But getting back to my grandfather, did you know that he was one of the first black men to run for office in Alabama? True. He ran for the border . . . and made it!

And there's more about my family background that you probably didn't know. Like where I was born. I was born in this country. My father was born in this country. My grandfather was born here and my great-grandfather was brought here . . . in chains! But they caught his black ass, as he was fishing too close to the river.

As far as my ancestry goes, just take a good look at my face; you got to know someone back there got integrated. See those lips? Thin, huh? Can hardly taste bar-b-que.

I'm mixed, so I don't know who to hate. But if I got to hate something, it's midgets and okra. But I really hate midgets. The little bastards breathe on your fly!

It's like the person who is a victim. Like recently, the surgeon general said that cigarette smoking was bad for your health. They waited until I was smoking over thirty years, then they're going to tell me that smoking is bad for my health! Well, if I don't have cancer now, then I got something that'll eat it up. Well, as I always say, you've got to die of something. You'd look funny as hell laying up in a hospital dying of nothing.

Malcolm X was a friend of mine and he was having a hard time getting people to listen to him. So I suggested

REDD FOXX

that he try telling the people a funny incident. Before you get down to the nitty-gritty, get them to laugh first. Then, when you've got their attention, drop your spiel on them. He tried it and it worked.

I've worked over thirty years in clubs and they were not the best years. I had to learn to contend with eventualities. As they come up, you can't anticipate what's going to happen, but you learn how to cope so that nothing could floor you.

Another thing a comic has got to do is learn to utilize the things around him. It helps you to become aware, and your performance will benefit from it. Comedy is a science. It looks easy because it seems that all you do is walk on a stage in a comedy act without having to train or rehearse. All you need in comedy is subject matter.

So, to most people just starting out, they think it's a snap—until they come up against their first hostile audience. This either makes them or breaks them. It's the way a young comic overcomes his first obstacle. It also teaches him that there's a lot of people out there that are funny; but it takes work to become a comedian.

I'm basically a night person. That's why I'm best in a night-club. In Las Vegas, I'm at home. Sure, my shows are rated triple-X (for mature audiences) but that's only because my image there is the opposite of Sanford. On TV I play a sour-tempered lovable old goat—a real grandfather image that everyone can relate to.

Not everyone relates to me in Las Vegas. I've seen people walk out in the middle of my act. But that's understandable. My topics are adult, and not everyone is adult, even though they may be fifty years old.

The one thing I don't like about television is that you got to work in the daytime. I prefer the late hours. To me, daylight is something to sleep by. I wake up at night and I'm as alert as a bat. When I wake up I like to see the dreary look of twilight. Sometimes when it's gloomy, I just sink

Redd Foxx and Admirer

Scatman Crothers with Redd Foxx (as Fred Sanford)

REDD FOXX

right down and enjoy it. I really reach my peak at around eleven o'clock when I got a glass in my hand (it used to be scotch, now it's water, since I stopped drinking), standing in front of a mike. I'm at home.

Of course, I appreciate television because of its power. It enabled me to become a box-office draw. I don't underestimate the tube, but if I can have my druthers, I'd druther be in Las Vegas playing Keno and working less.

In Vegas I can work one weekend and make more dough than Sanford can pay me for a whole week. But, it's like I say, I'm no idiot. Television made me famous. And it would be a dream come true if we only went to work at night. But the way it is—working days in Los Angeles and weekend nights in Las Vegas—it ain't too good. It beats going to Las Vegas every weekend as a tourist and losing dough and not making dough. This way, I go to Las Vegas to work and, even if I do gamble, I got a salary in Las Vegas to gamble with.

There is no place in the world like Las Vegas. It's the swingingest place in the world. It's the place and the home of the superstars. In Las Vegas, we got Frank Sinatra, Sammy Davis, Jr., Don Rickles, Dean Martin, Shecky Greene, and Bill Cosby. If they're big, they're in Las Vegas.

Oh yeah, and there's me! Like I say, I play me, not Sanford. I've been Redd Foxx for over fifty years and I've only been Sanford for five. 'Nough said!

But I give the prudish folks a chance to change their minds. I tell them, "Don't grumble and stay. Grumble and be on your merry way. Your ass ain't glued to that seat. Bye!"

Then there's my other favorite ringside bit. If I spot a pretty lady sitting there right in front and she's with a man, I'll say to the man:

"Sir, is this your wife? Got kids?" If the answer is yes to both questions, I'll say, "Sir, you're a motherfucker! (Never thought a black cat could call you a motherfucker and you'd laugh about it, did you?)"

REDD FOXX

But it was the same way during the pretelevision days of my career. There was always the question, should Redd Foxx clean up his act? It started to get to me so bad that I actually did it a couple of times. I started to believe all that crap about how it would keep me off the mass media.

But each time I did, I felt sorry about it. I hated the thought that I was selling out. I figured, shit, I'm an adult, so why couldn't I say what I wanted to? What's words, anyway, 'specially when they're not true.

What turned me around for good was my records. They was being sold "under the counter." And mostly to kids. I used to like to tell my club audience that while they were there listening to me, their kids were safe and snug at home—listening to my records. Sometimes when the parents would tell me that they were shocked at what I said on stage, I would tell them, "Hey, I don't care if you don't like me. I appeal to the kids. Besides, I don't give a damn if you're not my fans; you ain't gonna be here long no way."

I don't advise young comedians to start off with material that might keep them from getting a job. Young new comics can get turned around because they think they can get up there and say motherfucker and try to get laughs. I've been asked many times by new kids who want to know why they can't be accepted when they do it. Instead of laughs, the people feel hostile toward them.

I understand what they're going through. What a young dude don't understand is that I never call nobody a motherfucker. I use the word, but I don't call nobody anything. There's a difference.

I don't want to be a leader, either. I could, but I just don't want to be one. I don't dig no organizations, 'specially those that want you to give up the pig, grunt, feet, tail, hogs, maws, fatback, and greenbacks.

Hey, do you know why money is green? Jews pick it before it gets ripe.

REDD FOXX

I used that gag in a club once and some guy had the nerve to say I'm anti-Semitic. Ain't that something? You know I ain't anti-Semitic—I'm Baptist. I used to be a Catholic, but when I found out I couldn't be pope, I said, "Fuck 'em!"

This is how jokes follow jokes, even in conversation. Each topic leads to another without planning it. This is what keeps comedy fresh. Dig? Like this:

"These broads today are asking for a hundred dollars a whap. If I thought I had anything on me worth $100, I'd cut it off and bar-b-que it.

"I don't want to live with no broad, I just want to drop in for a while. But that's what you do with some of these hundred-dollar broads; you drop in . . . and in . . . and in!

"You ever be laying up with some broad and you're making it, shooting your best shot? She'd be just laying there, so I shout, 'Do somethin', bitch. Belch!'

"I don't want no white woman. When you see me with a white woman, I'm holding her for the police. I ain't stupid, either. I prefer Elizabeth Taylor to Shirley Chisholm. I even prefer Richard Burton to Shirley Chisholm. Just like you white cats prefer Lena Horne to Eleanor Roosevelt."

This country revolted from England because of the lack of communication. We said, "No taxation without representation, etc. etc." But let's be honest for once. We broke from England because we felt and smelled a sense of freedom that England did not possess. We found honesty here, and that ain't all that we found here. We found a wealth of natural resources that were unheard of in the old country.

But we fought for our freedom. We fought our asses off. Like the time General Custer made the famous statement during the heat of battle: "Where the hell did all these Indians come from?"

And in our fight for freedom, it was just as tough. I remember the time when I was fighting in the war. I was

fighting so hard, I backed up all the way into a general. He asked me, "Why are you backing up, soldier?" I answered, "I am backing up, sir, because I cannot fly."

These are some of the big things I like to comment on—I mean, world affairs. Like the Chinese situation. You gotta watch those Chinese. Don't worry about black folks. It's the Chinese. Did you know there's 800 million of them? Eight hundred million! Face it, white friends, they've out-fucked us!

America is going to need all the help it can get when we fight them—'specially at night. And God knows I tried to help. I even went so far as to marry an Oriental. I married the enemy. Well, if you can't beat 'em, fuck 'em!

Then there was the time Nixon tried to tell the American public that he lied, but he didn't have the nerve. He'd been stonewalling it so long that he didn't know the truth if it hit him in the face. Had he been able to just face the American public and say to them, "Look, I fucked up, I'm sorry," everyone would have loved him. But he had lost his ability to be honest.

Take the time former Secretary of Agriculture Earl Butz was supposed to have made a statement unbecoming to a public figure. It was a shocking statement because he was supposed to know better than to exercise such execrable taste.

His statement was simply this: "Black people are easily pleased. All they like are tight vaginas, loose shoes and Cadillacs." That statement cost him his gig. Richard Pryor says the same thing on his record Bicentennial Nigger and they buy his records like mad.

And don't get mad when I tell a Polish joke; just think back when you used to tell those nigger stories to your white friends. Or when you pass the homes in the suburbs and you'd see a little black jockey on all the lawns. I tell my black friends, don't get mad; go and get yourself a little white jockey and put it on your lawn.

It's our double standard of lifestyles. It's all right to think racial things—but it's wrong to say it. Says who? I say

REDD FOXX

enjoy yourself. Enjoy the moment. Don't come around here and watch my show and tell me what I'm doing is wrong. Or tell me what's wrong or right. "The Lord sees your Christian ass sitting here in Las Vegas getting drunk. Get drunk. Go out and do something wrong!" I say. "Puke in the taxi on the ride back to your hotel. That's the trouble with America; we've forgotten how to puke!"

Sure, I use the word <u>nigger</u> all the time. But I say niggers is holding the black people back. It don't mean black at all. In the dictionary, <u>nigger</u> is described as a person who is shiftless and lazy. Well, if that's the case, there must be some white niggers, too. If you don't believe it, look at TV's "Hee Haw": "Hey, Ezra, is it rainin' outside?" "I don't know. Call the dog in and see if he's wet."

You hear that all black people look alike; you hear that all the time. I say no way. White folks, you're the ones that all look alike. Think about it. You're just white. Now take us: we come in all colors—brown, mocha, burnt almond, yellow, mellow, light, bright, and damn near white! But the one thing that bugs me is this: people come in all colors—white, black, brown, yellow—but there's no negro in the crayon box!

I don't allow comps to my shows. (Letting people in for free complimentary passes.) Lots of people think I should do like the other acts that play Vegas—comps, freebies. They got to be kidding. I am not going to do it.

Look at it this way, the only money I've got coming is from the door. It's my livelihood. I've got to pay me and my show out of what comes from the door. If at the end of the night I'm stuck with a lot of comps, where in the hell is the money going to come from . . . my pocket? Well, they got to be crazy. If your friends don't want to pay to see you, you know you've lost the enemy. When I go into a place, I don't get no kind of guarantee—only what I can pull in at the door. It's my place of work. Do any of you give your work away? Hell, no. Well, why in hell should I give my art away?

REDD FOXX

It took me forty years of sweat, working under the worst conditions to get there. By the time you're able to make a halfway decent living, you've got to turn around and cut your money up in so many ways that some stars wind up all their life paying someone else for their talent.

Lots of people wonder why I don't have a manager. I don't need a manager. I've managed myself all these years, so why do I need someone to tell me how to do my job? I know, they say a man shouldn't wear too many hats. Well, I've been out here and I know my facts from personal experience.

I remember when managers and so-called good friends would say to me, "Clean up your act or you're not going to be able to get on television doing the kind of act you do." It's not a case of doing a dirty act; I don't consider myself as being a dirty act even now. I feel I'm an adult show. I use the words <u>fuck</u>, <u>shit</u>, <u>motherfucker</u> in my talks, but no one resents it because I don't say it with any hostility. I say it and I laugh. And the people laugh. They know they want to say that at that particular time.

That's the secret of being accepted. When I explain to the audience the use of the word <u>shit</u> and show where in the average household the word is used so that it brings a laugh, they love me because I've said the truth.

"Remember the first time when your wife put her first meal before you and you said, 'What's this shit?'" Now, what's going through the average man's head at that time is an incident that has happened, and that's why the statement evokes a laugh. Association. It's how comedy is accepted.

Risqué comedy has been with us always. Burlesque used the sex symbol for laughs—strippers, along with sight gags of girls with their boobs hanging out and tight skirts that showed a broad's ass as she walked.

Look at Vegas—the town of tits and ass. Everywhere you go in that town, broads are walking around showing it all, letting it all hang out. All I do when I'm on stage there is say what the guys are thinking when they're watching the broads.

REDD FOXX

When I tell the story about the broad walking up to me and asking me for a hundred dollars, like it was a Spam sandwich, I'm not joking and every dude in that room knows it. That's why I come back with, "She forced me to say shit (laugh) and fuck you (laugh) and get out of my face! (roar)." Anyone in Las Vegas can really associate that statement.

And this one, too: "I tell a broad I just want to drop in for a little while. I don't want to move in. And some of those hundred-dollar broads, you can really drop in . . . plop (laugh). I was humping this old broad and I said, 'Is it in?' She said, 'Yes.' I said, 'Well, pack a little pussy around it!'"

It's the gesture that gets the laugh. Again, association. Every dude in that room has had a similar experience. I'm not dirty for dirty's sake. That's what I try to explain to young comedians. Don't strap yourselves with dirty material because all you think you got to say is some words that will make people laugh. It will have just the opposite effect. It will make it difficult for you to get ahead.

In comedy, it takes a long time to create an image. Without the image, the comedy doesn't ring true. It's only when it's true is it truly funny. Black folks' comedy is built out of reality. It's the heartbreaking things that happen to black people, that make our comedy so basic.

In using the word motherfucker, I show how under similar circumstances anybody would use the word. Try standing by a car door, and the door is slammed on your fingers, and you yell, "Watch it, motherfucker! You got my motherfuckin' finger. Help!" Enough said.

At no time do I use a phrase that's not used in everyday life, because that's what I represent—life.

What I do is not new with me. I've cut fifty-two record albums. I must have been saying something to be able to have fifty-two albums. I talk about sex, because that's what people have—sex. Look, we did something to get here. Ain't nobody drawed us. "People have sex. That's why I say, 'I'm mixed. I have to be. You didn't think I was a semialbino, did you? My parents were mixed, but she had me. It's better than being left at a picnic—on a Kleenex."

REDD FOXX

Truth, that's all I got going for me. It's what paid off. If I had compromised and done what someone else told me, today I'd be where they are—asking me for a job.

I've worked all my life. I don't know no other way. People wonder why I work as much as I do. Simple. I get paid for it and paid well. But I also like what I'm doing. And remember, whenever you are doing something you like, then it's no longer work. You see, I'm fortunate. I can get onstage and say the things that bug me when I'm offstage. It gives me a pulpit to air my grievances and get a laugh out of it, too. Comedy represents the other side of you. We're all two persons—the one we show the world and the real one we've got to live with.

Redd Foxx offstage is the one who stays in his room. I never venture out too much. I'm a real homebody, but I can get onstage and say the things that give people hangups. It's one way of having an outlet. It balances things out. Listen, Reverend Ike gets up there and tells them what they want to hear. They throw money at his feet. Well, I'm like Ike. Give me my shit while I'm here now.

People are crazy. Like my friend Timmie Rogers said in his song, "Everybody wants to go to heaven." Then when you die, they lower your ass into the ground and some bastard comes along and builds a condominium over your ass.

Comedy is like preaching. I could have been a preacher. Religion is strange. It's like the story about the crippled man who had so much faith that he threw away his crutches . . . and there he was crawling around trying to get them back.

When I see a fat dude in the audience, I always try to tell him, "Man, do something about that weight. When did you last see your weenie?" This is a sight gag. It always works, because the man is put on the defensive. Now, if I see where he might resent it, I say to him, "Now, watch it, we both carry knives." This immediately softens him with a laugh.

250

REDD FOXX

Laughter is what it's all about. If I said something on-stage and the people didn't laugh, I wouldn't use it again. It's because it brings laughter that I say what I say. I guess somewhere in the past, certain stereotypes must have stuck with me, because there are things I still resent that smack in the way of "Tomming." Blackface comedy, bucking eyes, I've always tried to stay away from it. Black men only like Cadillacs? I wouldn't buy one. I bought me a Rolls-Royce.

A toast, ladies and gentlemen! Everybody please lift their glass.

"A gentleman shouldn't argue with a lady . . . he should dicker."

African humor: "What do you find in an elephant's trunk? Two six-foot buggers."

Mexican humor: "Why does it have hair around it? To keep it from looking like a taco."

These are breakers. They allow you to go in another direction. It keeps you from traveling at the same rate on every show. Material must always sound fresh, even though you have done it over and over many times. I don't go for the routine sound, line for line as it's written, because in standup comedy, you've got to learn to wing it.

One of the best of this type is Jackie Gayle. He's bright with what's happening. He's always funny. He never uses line-for-line comedy. It's the secret for success in the nightclub.

Bill Cosby is another one who is very successful with his formula. He works as if it's being done for the first time. It's the way to keep material fresh. It's when your experiences become a part of your life that you can be comfortable talking about it.

Now the difference with Richard Pryor is that his are routines that have been routinely refined. But they are acting pieces. When Richard is Richard, he's a serious person. It's the characters he can slip in and out of that makes Richard's performance brilliant.

REDD FOXX

Now, I don't use characterizations. I'm doing the other side of me when I'm onstage. Life is a fuckup. I just point it out to the people and they see it, too.

I think that the basic reason that people think that Richard and I are considered stylists of this comedy is that he's a comedic actor and I'm a comedian. He does things funny and I say things funny. He's like a son to me. I can get into his head. We both have a lot of respect for each other. I think he's the finest piece of talent on the scene today and deserves his successes. His wino routine is a typical example. It's a brilliant piece of acting. He's done it many times, although you know the climax and you almost know the routine. "You Got To Wash Your Ass" is a developed routine. It grew. Most people have experienced this embarrassment but just think how many marriages might have been saved by people being honest with each other.

People are funky. Today, kids talk about getting funky. Today it's a dance—the funky chicken. I remember when it had nothing to do with a beat; it was an aroma. It was Grandpa's funky drawers, with the tobacco stains in the seat. One time when I was a kid, I was playing hide-and-seek and I hid in the clothes closet where Grandma kept the dirty clothes. It was fuuuunnnnnkkkkyyyy! I hurried and gave myself up. Now, that's funky. And nothing is worse than laying beside someone and they are fuuunnnnkkkkyyy!

That's why I say, "You got to wash your ass!" You can let your armpits go a couple of days, but not your ass. Of course, this isn't said in public. Of course not, but isn't it true? Some people's ass is funky, and someone should tell them. I did.

No one resents the truth. They're shocked at the truth, but when they think about it, they say, "Yeah, the cat's right."

REDD FOXX

The old way they did the gag by telling about the man who brought home a skunk. His wife was mad and wanted him to take the skunk out of their bedroom. "What about that smell?" she asked. He answers, "Let him get used to it like I did."

Today he would say, "Why don't you wash your ass?" Truth. It will set you free. I've been set free but you've got to pay to see it. But, I promise you, I'll try to bring a little laughter into your lives. You might as well enjoy it now because when nuclear war comes, we will all be black 'cause heat will brown your meat. If you don't believe me, put your ass in the oven. Put it on broil and see if it don't brown your meat.

So laugh. When you laugh, the world laughs with you, but when you cry, that's your ass. Who gives a fuck?

It's great, after all these years, to see how my life was influenced by great performers in show business. You know, I've always loved real show business and Las Vegas has got real show business. Here in Las Vegas, it's the shows. If there were no shows here, this desert would dry up like the land. People come here because they know they're always going to see a good show and the world's greatest entertainers. I always wanted to be where real show business is, and it's here in Las Vegas.

When I think back to people like Bert Williams, who played the Ziegfeld Follies, I think of somebody who was real pioneer show business. Anyone who could portray emotion with all that gook on his face had to be a great artist.

Las Vegas used to be like Bert Williams. He couldn't get a ham sandwich if he walked into a place without his makeup. It used to be like that here. Black entertainers had to dress in trailers outside the casinos. I remember when Dinah Washington played here and they made the Queen dress in a trailer. Can you believe that shit? Boy, I can just imagine what it must have been like for a cat like Bert Williams! But he became a star in spite of everything.

REDD FOXX

I remember the first time I played before a segregated audience. It was at The Palace in New York and Slappy and I bombed so bad, I hurried up and went back to the ghetto.

The first time I came to Los Angeles, they were prejudiced as hell here. They didn't like the idea of a black man talking about sex. Everybody used to tell me, "Man, clean up your act. White people don't want a nigger talking dirty." I remember when I opened at the Basin Street East in New York, I went on and I did my usual routines. At the same time, I was doing the racetrack routine and another one that was on the records, "Fugg and Sugg." Those records sold like crazy, so naturally I had to do routines the audience expected of me. Well, after the show, I went to the john, and there was this dude on the telephone saying to someone, "He's the dirtiest thing I ever heard." Then he turns around and sees me standing there. I just gave him one of my best go-fuck-yourself looks and he got the message.

After that I went on doing me and have been doing me ever since. When I think back to how it was with me and I think of all those great comics that went before me, I know it was because they held the fort that I came along and was able to believe in me. I didn't have to compromise. There was a time when I didn't think I was going to make it. But I've got to give credit to Bert Williams. I often wonder about the blackface. It was my generation that insisted on the elimination of it. I knew I was never going to do it, but I guess it had an influence on me. I don't know if I would have been different if I had been around in those days, but I feel deep in my heart that I wouldn't have made a good blackface comedian.

I'm grateful that I made it, though. It feels great to know that there's something you do that the people like and respond to. I feel they want me to stay the way I am. I am not going to change. It's like I always say, when the public knows your image, they want that. They don't want you becoming like some saint. They know I'm not a saint. I'm what they want to see—Redd Foxx, telling it like it is.

REDD FOXX

Television came too late for some of the great talents that went by the wayside. But maybe this book will let their memories live on. To the great comedians all over the world—some gone, and those that are still around—to all of you, I didn't want to leave anyone out, but if there are some we didn't reach, blame Norma. She did the research. I didn't have the time, but we did try to tell it like we heard it and knew it.

To Bert Williams, he gave us art. He made comedy with music, beautiful to see and listen to. I still have fond memories of him from his records.

Then there was the great team of Miller and Lyles, whose work was stolen by white dudes, Amos 'n' Andy. Anyway, they still had to come back to us because of television.

Who knows what would have happened if the world had seen John Mason and Dusty Fletcher. When I see Richard Pryor's drunk act, I think of Dusty Fletcher's drunk bit he did with a stepladder. No one has ever been his equal.

Then, of course, there was Pigmeat. He was in my time. I always saw him at the Apollo, the Howard in Washington, and the Royal in Baltimore—the Big League of the Chitlins Circuit.

Then there was the newer cats that started coming up. One of the funniest cats of all was Willie Lewis. He twirled the batons and was the first to do the balcony bit. He was the funniest guy around at one time.

We began to move out with Dick Gregory. That cat was funny until he took his causes serious. He committed himself to an idea that he believed in.

Then there came Bill Cosby, a great humorist. And my man, Flip Wilson. Flip always comes by to see me now.

And there's Stu Gilliam, the ventriloquist-turned-stand-up comedian, and George Kirby and Irwin C. Watson, who has the best West Indian accent going.

And, of course, there's my ex-partner, Slappy White. We came a long way together, traveling the rough roads as well as the smooth ones. And without the Queen, Dinah

Washington, in the beginning, probably neither one of us would have made it.

Then there was the wonderful Moms Mabley. I loved her. She was very special to me. Moms is gone, but she'll always live on in my heart.

So will Godfrey Cambridge. I worked with him in the picture Cotton Comes to Harlem. He was a great comedian and a great actor.

We wanted to interview everybody in doing this book, but in case we did leave someone out, we're going to say to every one of you that today comedy is king. People need to laugh now more than ever and as long as there are cats like those we've mentioned still around, comedy will be around. Keep them laughing.

BLACK
LANGUAGE

BLACK LANGUAGE

Identification and communication are two essential assets for a people. No people can have a future without knowing their past. The Africans' background was all but obliterated when they were brought to this country. Since they were not allowed to associate with other slaves, and since they spoke many different tongues, anyway, they had to use whatever other means they had to communicate with their peers. This came about in their songs and in the phrases they used to talk to their brothers and sisters.

In the early building of this country, various ethnic groups were thrown together and had a big influence on the English language spoken here. The Africans heard words pronounced by people from England, Scotland, Ireland. It was confusing to the ear; the sound was as foreign to them as were their own languages, which they were not allowed to use. Hence, their language came out as a conglomeration of what they heard. Then, to add to this potpourri, they developed their own kind of communication by creating a language of their own that later became an important part of America's "slanguage."

They also used songs to express themselves, for example, "The Birth of the Blues":

Woke up this mornin'
Wid de blues hangin' over mah head
Woke up this mornin'
Wid de blues hangin' over mah head,
If I feel like dis tomorrow,
Den I wish dat I was dead.

The blues is as much a part of America as slavery and white folks. It was this strange relationship that became the very root of the blues.

Body language was expressed in dance form. The dancing that the blacks developed came from what they observed. For example, the Irish jig later became known as tap dancing. Another carry-over from the plantation days

BLACK LANGUAGE

was the strut (slave masters found it amusing to see their slaves dress up in their discarded clothes and "strut" around proudly); this later became the cakewalk:

Strutting down the avenue,
Without a single thing to do.

On the plantations the slaves used their hands for rhythmic accompaniment, stroking their thigh and flipping back the hand to hit the shoulder, all the while singing a patter to the beat. During plantation days, this was called doing the juba. Today, it's called hambone. Every black kid in America knows "Hambone":

Hambone, Hambone, have you heard?
Papa's gonna buy you a mockingbird.
If that mockingbird don't sing,
Papa's gonna buy you a diamond ring;
If that diamond ring don't shine,
Papa's gonna buy you a bottle of wine.
Hambone, Hambone . . .

Then the clapping picks up and the rhythm is now a slap and a clap.

Slang became a vital tool for the blacks to be able to communicate with one another. The slang talk and the body language were the two ingredients that enabled them to excel in pantomime. Their movements could paint pictures, à la one of today's more prominent comedians, Richard Pryor. His talk was a simple melding of words, dialect, and slow expression, which was sometimes called pidgin English.

When Miller and Lyles were appearing in vaudeville, their act was called "Blessed with Ignorance." They did a dialect that was called "mutilatin' the language." When Bert Williams did his interpretation, it was called "actin' the nigger." Their slow speech and exaggerated drawl kept audiences in stitches.

BLACK LANGUAGE

Today's black men use a sign language when they meet on the streets. This greeting is called "the dap" and it works like this: If you are too far apart to touch, then you close your hand to make a fist, the sign of the brother. It says to the other, "Get it together." It's the same clenched fist that the African warrior used when he carried his spear. Remove the spear and what's left? The clenched fist or the sign of the brother. It spread like forest blaze around the world.

Another version of the dap is the turning up of the palms to the other and letting the hands be touched. Open palms, "I'm a friend"; the clenched fist, "Togetherness."

Words play a role in greetings as well. For example, "Hey, black, gimme some dap; zap, zap, zap!" It's their identity. It means together forever, you and me.

Whenever the greeting was on the street, the words would always begin with, "Man," "Hey, man," "My man," or "My main man." In analyzing the use of the word man, it's been said that the black man so resented being called boy by his master, whatever his age, that man was universally adopted.

A black man in his prime was called "boy," but an old black man was always called "uncle," i.e., "Uncle Tom." This also became a sore spot for all black men; consequently, the word man became doubly important as part of their speech.

Words of the ghettos spilled out to every corner of American society, mainly because of the acceptance of black music (jazz) by white musicians.

Back in the forties when jazz guitarist Slim Gaillard was putting out hit after hit on Atomic Records in Los Angeles, a little pocket handbook known as Slim Gaillard's Vout-o-Renee Dictionary hit the streets. Gaillard, being a master of the double-talk/double-sing, had more fun with his own language than anyone on the scene at the time, and many of his verbal concoctions caught on. For example:

BLACK LANGUAGE

Caresser	Arm
Caro-spon-ee	Letter
Cheap gold	Copper
David	Beard
Dig	Think, understand
Gold o-reenee	Eagle
Goose feathers	Snow
Head pills	Hail
H-twenty	Water
Jing	Bell
Loot	Money
Main stem	Mother
Mello-o-REEN-EE	Wonderful, fine
Mell-o-ROON-EE	Same as above
Para-suit-O	Umbrella
Puti-puti	Rhythm
Rake	Comb
Reet	Right, yes, okay
Root	Same as reet
San-witch-ee	Between
Shovel	Spoon
Slim-o-ree-nee	Sharp
Tackbeater	Shoemaker
Ugh	Heavy
Vite-e-cee	Oranges
Vout-a	Minute
Vout-o	Hour
Vout-o-reen-ee	Good performance, good music
Walker	Foot
Web-stomp	Duck
Weight-watcher	Salad
Yep-rock	Food, specifically grape leaves stuffed with rice and lamb

BLACK LANGUAGE

The dictionary even listed words for numbers (ax for six, octa for eight, and so on). Gaillard contributed greatly toward standardizing the street language of that generation.

The way blacks and whites referred to each other varied according to what part of the country they came from. Blacks from the West called a white man "redneck," while blacks from the East called the white man "pecker wood." Blacks from the city called the white "honky." In Harlem during the 1920s and 1930s, whites were called "ofay."

To some the word nigger was offensive, but the word is now as much a part of the English language as ain't.

As an example of this, there is the story about the white man who goes into the offices of the NAACP and asks to speak to the "head nigger." The receptionist is appalled at the statement and sends for the vice-president. The vice-president comes out into the reception area and expresses shock at what the receptionist has just told him. "Yeah, that's right," the white man repeats, "I want to speak to the head nigger." The vice-president, in all his eloquence, says, "Sir, you are in the offices of the National Association for the Advancement of Colored People. How dare you come in here and make such a request!" The white man, completely unperturbed, says, "Look, I've got a check here for $25,000 that I am to deliver to the head nigger. Now do I see him or not?" The vice-president quickly responds, "Yasir, I'll go get the head nigger right away!"

The question is always asked, "Why do black people talk the way they do?"

Some linguists hypothesize that it is "Because they have thick lips."

Black linguists demur, "Say that again, turkey, and I'll go up 'side yo' head!"

While there doesn't seem to be any written explanation of how the phrase up 'side yo' head got started, it is generally agreed that it is a variation on the term upside-down. In other words: "I'll put yo' head where yo' feet is, turkey!"

BLACK LANGUAGE

In Fran Ross's glossary of black terminology, in <u>Titters</u>, the first collection of humor by women, definitions to the following terms are listed:

<u>Bad</u>, as in "Man, that's baaaad!" It's the emphasis on the word <u>bad</u> that means the opposite—it's the <u>best</u>.

<u>Jive-mother</u>, someone who is a liar, and a no-good.

<u>Turkey</u>, a gentler type of put-down.

<u>I've been screwed</u>, someone has taken you in whatever manner that wasn't good.

<u>That's saying sumpin'</u>, something that's good.

<u>Tough titty</u>, you got a problem.

<u>Stone</u>, way-out, freaked out on something.

<u>Out of his skull</u>, stone crazy, nuts.

When is the term <u>nigger</u> used in an offensive way? This has always puzzled many white people because they wonder why it is that blacks use the word more than anyone. This is true. Blacks do use the word more than anyone because today they have the word <u>black</u> to identify themselves.

<u>Nigger</u> no longer refers to a people; it's an attitude. "Actin' the nigger" means acting like a damn fool. This can mean anyone, but it is used to mean to act like a darky, a coon, a buffoon.

Now that black people have a sense of identity, they too can hear the word and not cringe. The word <u>Negro</u> at one time referred to a black person. Now that he no longer identifies with "Negro," the black has taken the word and made it part of his humor.

As Redd Foxx says, "People are all colors, white, black, brown, yellow, mellow . . . ain't no negro in the crayon box!"

Dick Gregory's first book was called <u>Nigger</u>. In dedicating it to his mother, he told her, "Everytime they call me nigger, remember, mama, they are paying me."

BLACK LANGUAGE

When asked when he will stop using the word <u>nigger</u> in his act, Richard Pryor answered, "When my characters stop using it. Until then, nigger, get out of my face!"

The black comedian of today uses the language of the streets and in doing his characterizations, he speaks the same way. The term <u>right on</u> came from the streets and gained instant national popularity in the early seventies. It's still in wide use today.

The word <u>fuck</u> is used frequently on the stage today, and the audience reaction to it is much different than it used to be. In his routine in Las Vegas, Redd Foxx says, "Fuck Kate Smith!" and then he repeats, "All together now, fuck Kate Smith!" And the audience yells back, "Fuck Kate Smith!" This reaction shows that people are joining in, not because they have something against Kate Smith, but they're shedding their inhibitions and letting themselves go, at least for the moment. When Redd Foxx says it, he doesn't mean he has a dislike for Kate Smith, it means he's poking fun at what is sacred.

But the word <u>fuck</u> is heard quite extensively among Americans today. It's a word that has many meanings. Most of the time, it's merely a release. "Oh, fuck!" "Go fuck yourself!" "Oh, fuck it!"

As Redd says, "Fuck ain't dirty . . . unless you don't wash up . . . and if you don't wash up, you're fuckin' dirty!"

Although the word <u>fuck</u> is not of black origin (it supposedly is an abbreviation of the words "for unknown carnal knowledge" and got into the language many centuries ago), there is no doubt that black street language has spilled over to every walk of life in our society today, thus making the American English language that much more (if you'll pardon the expression) colorful.